Extraordinary
Freedom

Extraordinary Freedom

Buddhist Wisdom for Modern Times

Dana Marsh

Foreword by Anam Thubten

authorHOUSE®

AuthorHouse™
1663 Liberty Drive
Bloomington, IN 47403
www.authorhouse.com
Phone: 1-800-839-8640

Published by AuthorHouse   10/27/2014

ISBN: 978-1-4969-4688-1 (sc)
ISBN: 978-1-4969-4689-8 (e)

Library of Congress Control Number: 2014918445

Contents

Foreword vii

Introduction ix

Chapter 1   Getting Out of the Pot 1

Chapter 2   A Rare and Precious Opportunity 15

Chapter 3   Freedom from the Jail of Thoughts 25

Chapter 4   Healing the Cancer of Delusion 35

Chapter 5   Adversity Is Not the Problem 43

Chapter 6   Tea with My Teachers 55

Chapter 7   An Unencumbered Life 65

Chapter 8   No I in You 73

Chapter 9   Dive into the Ocean of Love 81

Chapter 10 It's Enough! 89

Chapter 11 Living with an Awakened Heart 101

Chapter 12 The Extraordinary in the Ordinary 111

Notes 119

Foreword

It's truly delightful to see Dana Marsh's first book come into being. It was a pleasure for me to read it. Dana has been my good friend for many years. She is someone who lives what she teaches, and she constantly embodies love and insight. Her teachings have already helped many people find a way to open their hearts and gain a deeper understanding about themselves and the world around them. This has to do with the fact that she's practiced Buddhism for many years, and her good intentions are the foundation of her work.

Buddhism is a more than two-thousand-year-old spiritual tradition. It is rich with profound wisdom and transformative methodologies. Yet, some of the language can be too esoteric and removed from our daily lives, and people may have a very hard time connecting to it. This has been a concern among many progressive Buddhist teachers and scholars. There is a fine line to making it approachable without diluting its depth. We all know that this is a daunting task. I feel that Dana is doing this job remarkably well. You'll find this by reading her book.

Someone from a traditional monastery in the East may not easily recognize this as a Buddhist text, yet Dana has expressed the essential point of the Buddha's teachings.

Dana is deeply connected to the Nyingma lineage of Tibetan Buddhism. She has a great love for the teachings of the great masters of Tibet, such as Machik Labdrön, Longchenpa, and so forth. She has the skill to convey their wisdom in a contemporary form that still has the potency to move the hearts of others. Her presence is a gift to many of us.

I'd like to congratulate her on the publication of this book where, readers will find both gentleness and directness. As a Dharma teacher, this is also who she is. She is loving and compassionate without compromising the truth that must be pointed out. Many people need a book like this that is simple in its language and profound in its meaning. My wish is that many people will benefit from its life-changing messages.

Anam Thubten
San Francisco Bay Area
April 19, 2014

Introduction

Sometimes we may feel as though we are hacking our way through a jungle of thoughts and emotions, stumbling upon steep and hidden cliffs of anxiety, and narrow trails covered with thorns of worry. It may seem that all of our attempts to get out of this jungle lead us back to where we started. Striving for long-term joy becomes one big circle of sweating, climbing, and slipping back again and again. We may reach great heights of bliss every now and then, but then challenges arise and we find ourselves sliding back down the slippery slope of dissatisfaction. It is a curious place to find ourselves in a landscape lush with hope and fear, thick with judgment, and maybe even blooming with self-hatred.

We may be well acquainted with this territory, the jungle of a confused and untamed mind. Often people think, *Is that all it is—an untamed mind?* All I can say is we underestimate its incredible power. An untamed mind is more harmful than a wild elephant in a market. It rushes from one thing to another, creating havoc in every direction. Running wildly from this place may be your first response, but it seems no matter how fast we run, we can't outrun ourselves.

Thankfully, it is possible to find freedom in the midst of the jungle. The Buddha and many beings since have been able to transform their relationship to life's hardships and joys. As going into any jungle requires physical courage, the inward journey requires inner courage. For some the journey is easy, and for others it is more difficult. It really depends on how openhearted, diligent, and willing we are to let go of everything (metaphorical nakedness), just be, and let the noise of the mind alone. We all have times when we feel completely inadequate, times when we barely hold on, times when our hearts are broken and we despair.

I'm personally familiar with this struggle, and this book is about how to go beyond habitual patterns to change our relationship to both our inner world and the outer world and to ultimately go beyond suffering. Unfortunately, habitual mental patterns often go unrecognized, and it isn't until we look inward that they bubble up like a hidden spring into our consciousness. This is actually good news, because when we have the chance to see how these patterns impact us we can make the necessary changes. By looking inside, we can eventually liberate ourselves by undoing the mental chains that bind us.

Siddhartha Gautama, who later became known as the Buddha, which means "Awakened One," laid out a path that can lead us from the prison of confused and untamed minds. The profound teachings of the Buddha are referred to as the Dharma. Putting these teachings into effect is the path. To walk this path involves change. However, it does not mean there is a need for a personality overhaul. Instead, it means we change the way we respond to the world around and within us. This isn't a willy-nilly sort of change; it is based on Buddhist wisdom.

Putting these teachings into effect in our lives does not require blind acceptance. Buddhism is an invitation to inquire within ourselves. It invites us to look at our experiences, including our thoughts, concepts, emotions, and beliefs. Through such an inquiry, there is often an opening and insight that changes the way we interact with everything.

Walking the path of the Dharma is a moment-by-moment practice. We do formal practices, like sitting meditation, but practice also includes working with our mind and seeing what is going on within throughout each day. When we do this, we discover the choice to respond to both the forces outside us and the ones inside us in a different way. We become less and less reactive to life. Through becoming conscious of our inner world, we have the opportunity to transform our lives. The wisdom we need is already within us; it is our true nature. Although we may not have access to it at this moment, it is there nonetheless. By practicing living in awareness, we discover this for ourselves. Awareness is the key that can unlock the door to our hearts, and when our hearts open, our lives also open like a lotus blossoming in the mud. We can be liberated from a confused mind and live in the light of awareness. The heavy burden that each of us carries can be dropped, and we can live a life free from the chains that bind us.

When engaging with the Dharma, it is helpful to let go of, or suspend, old concepts, beliefs, and judgments about who we are and how we think things are in this world. Instead, we open our hearts to the possibility that we aren't seeing our experiences clearly. Things are not as they appear to be. For example, a block of stone to the untrained eye is just a rock. However, to someone like Michelangelo, a stone is seen as much more. It is said that when asked how he would carve an elephant, Michelangelo indicated that he would take a large piece of stone and take away everything that was not the elephant.[1] Like this, maybe we can try to see ourselves as already complete, marvelous masterpieces. In order to reveal this in our consciousness, we will need to try on a new way of seeing our experiences and our relationship to them. Then the extraordinariness of life and the extraordinariness that we are will reveal itself, and the chains that hold us to old hardened views will break.

1

Getting Out of the Pot

The parable of the boiling frog describes how researchers compared the responses of frogs in two different experiments. In the first scenario, researchers placed a frog into a pot of boiling water. Without hesitation and regardless of the water level, the frog immediately acted on instinct and jumped to safety. In the second scenario, a frog was put into a pot of water, but this time the water temperature began as comfortable and nonthreatening. Researchers then gradually raised the temperature and waited for the frog to realize it was in danger and take appropriate action. But this never happened. Although the frog displayed sporadic moments of pain and discomfort, it did nothing. It continued to endure, adapt, and withstand the intolerable environment. The frog became increasingly lethargic and less responsive until it died.[2]

We too are often slowly boiled in the waters of conditioning, stress, anger, anxiety, worry, and fear and often don't know that our situation is dire. Instead of changing the way we live our lives, we continue, oblivious to the rising heat, until we meet our demise. Thankfully, if you are reading this book, you have noticed the heat and wish to jump out of the pot and into the cool waters of peace.

Your situation may not seem critical because the heat has been rising slowly. Sometimes it seems easier to stay with what we know rather than put forth the effort to venture into new territory. Staying in the pot seems okay; we really don't know that it will get hotter—or do we? We may think, *If only I were a better swimmer, prettier, skinnier, more muscular, smarter, or a funnier frog, I could change my situation.* So we swim around in the ever-warming pot, spending years trying to make ourselves better, worthy of life and love. As the temperature increases, we may start to worry and fret, complaining to everyone about the situation, blaming the universe for our troubles. We become lethargic, depressed, anxious, and hopeless, because no matter what we do, it doesn't seem to help. The temperature continues to rise even with all of our mental efforts to control the situation.

Does the water feel a little bit warm to you? Are you ready to jump, or do you prefer a new bathing suit so you can enjoy the Jacuzzi-like warmth of the pot?

You may ask, *What do I do? How can I become happy if it is not through the material world?* First, let me clarify that happiness is a shallow cousin to liberation. Happiness is a temporary state: it comes and goes based on what is happening in the world around us because it is dependent on conditions being the way we want them to be. We can be happy in the morning and sad by lunchtime. Liberation is independent of outer conditions; we are freed from negative states by unhooking ourselves from the chains of mental habits and habitual tendencies that bind us and make our lives difficult. When our minds are in turmoil, we can look within and we will find that we are resisting something. In other words, we want something—perhaps a thought, an emotion, or circumstance—to be different, to be like we want it to be.

This is the human condition; this is the source of our discontent. Of course it doesn't mean we shouldn't want things to be different than they are, but when we can't change life's circumstances and continue to pine for change, we increase the intensity of our discontent. It may even turn into powerful suffering. When we are unaware, thoughts and emotions form a groove in our consciousness and are replayed over and over again. In this case, habits rule us. However, when there is awareness, thoughts and emotions can arise and be seen for what they are, passing mental phenomena, and when not grasped, they don't leave a trace. Through awareness our lives are transformed. When encountering powerful emotions or negative circumstances, we may not overcome them, but we can learn to develop a nonacrimonious relationship with them. Mentally resisting our deep wounds seems to keep them more sensitive to the touch. By being willing to sit with the energy of what is arising, be it anger, sorrow, fear, or worry, we can come to find a place of peace and, hopefully, deep insight. If we don't hold onto expectations that life will get better or be different than it is right now, we might find moments of peace and joy arising in our consciousness.

To understand our lives, it helps to consider the culture we have been raised in and the assumptions we make about life itself. For example, in American culture in general, our most important values include wealth, prestige, individualism, material success, science and technology, and a strong work ethic, to name a few. Our focus is placed almost exclusively on the outer conditions of life—the material world. We try to manipulate the world to our whims, seeking something outside of us to fill us up and make our lives more meaningful. So we strive and work hard to capture the American dream. We are more centered on ourselves and our goals, with only a few, select people within our inner circle who receive the benefit of our efforts. "Every man for himself" seems like a plausible aphorism for life, but in reality, it hasn't worked out so well for us. There seems to be something missing in our lives that the material world can't give us.

Many people struggle with guilt for most of their lives and with regret at the end of their lives, wishing they could start over and do it all "right." Each of us will face the last moments of our lives with either regret or peace. Some of us will wait until the last minute to determine what is truly important, while others will consider this theme throughout their lives. Some may never get to the question at all, dying before they consider the lives they have lived. I'd like to suggest that we consider this question while we still have time to do so. In this way, we can make adjustments to our lives while we have sufficient energy and resources. Then we won't come to the end of our days filled with guilt and regret, but will feel that we have lived full and rich lives.

To find a reliable remedy for dissatisfaction, we will find help by looking at the lives of the great masters and saints of the past who spent quality time looking into themselves. They have all contributed to our understanding in different ways. Although these inspirational beings come from different traditions, the core of their insights are profoundly similar in nature. They found that in order to find meaning in life, we need to look inside ourselves. This is different than our normal approach of looking outward for something to bring meaning. It may even feel counterintuitive. Through looking at the landscape of our inner world, we will find the answers that we have been searching for in our outer experiences.

Carl Jung pointed out, "Your vision will become clear only when you can look into your own heart. Who looks outside, dreams; who looks inside, awakes."[3] When we take our focus away from the external world, even for a little while, and place it on the inner world, we will open the door to awaken to a new perspective, a new way of being in the world that is based on deep insight. In our everyday lives, we strive and struggle to gain comfort. Like greyhounds we chase after the ungraspable rabbit that is always just beyond our reach and are filled with a profound sense that we can't ever get enough. We live with a "wanting" mind, grasping for a bit more of this and a dab more of that. Indeed, our desire for material things is endless and dissatisfying. It is not too long after our desires are fulfilled that we find ourselves searching for something new. Our satisfaction is short-lived and lacks a sense of meaning. Although most of our basic needs are met, we may still find a subtle dissatisfaction lurking in the dark recesses of consciousness. We want people to change and situations to be different, and when this is the case, dissatisfaction has the tendency to manifest as anxiety, anger, hatred, jealousy, greed, false pride, and sorrow. It is easy to see how this dissatisfaction manifests in others and negatively impacts society.

Ultimately, we can't change anyone, no matter how good our intentions or how hard we try. So, the real work of our lives is completed by going within, because it is only ourselves that we can change. We can begin by examining our minds to see how we are the creators of our suffering. This may be obvious or more subtle and hard to see. It may take us some time to investigate our inner world to uncover the layers of habit energy, the force that drives us to react to what happens in our lives in a habitual fashion, and dissatisfaction that forms a veil blocking our view. Because we have not investigated our inner world, it may be difficult to see the coating of dissatisfaction lining the walls of all our experiences, like plaque built up on the walls of our arteries, slowly cutting off the vital flow of life energy. Beneath these layers of concepts, habits, and beliefs is a wellspring of joy, love, compassion, and wisdom.

Unless we take time to examine our lives, including our motivations, desires, attachments, and aversions, and see into their true nature, it will be quite difficult to get beyond a sense of lingering dissatisfaction or even downright suffering. Even when we seem to have everything, we may be caught in a web of dissatisfaction, spending a lot of hard work and money trying to alleviate it. It is easy to get caught up in the search for satisfaction in the wrong places as is seen in this anecdote entitled, *An American Story*.

A man goes to a doctor. "Doctor, I don't know what's wrong. I can't seem to stop worrying, I'm anxious, I can't sleep. I think I'm getting an ulcer…"

The doctor nods. "You do look exhausted. What's the matter?"

Patient answers, "I don't know. I'm not sure."

Doctor says, "Then tell me something about your life."

The man brightens up considerably and smiles. "Oh, everything is great. We have the best life. Honestly. We live in our own three-bedroom, two-bath home in a nice neighborhood in the suburbs, drive two new cars, have closets full of good clothes. Our three kids go to private schools. We eat out a couple of nights a week, belong to the country club, and have a condo in the mountains for skiing.

We had a great vacation last year in the Bahamas, and we're planning on going to Hawaii in two months."

The Doctor smiles, "My, that sounds wonderful!" the doctor says. "You have a wonderful life."

"Oh, we do, we do," the man says.

"Then what's your problem?" the Doctor asks.

The man shook his head. "Well, I'm not exactly sure. I think it might be that our income is only four hundred and sixty dollars a week."[4]

As you can see from this anecdote, even though life seems to be going well, there is often a silent but persistent dissatisfaction or fear that lingers in the dark recesses of consciousness. If we don't recognize the cause of our anxiety, we won't have a chance to overcome it. This same inner conflict is occurring in each of us. We may have smothered it nicely with hard work, hard play, and material success; however, the lack of satisfaction and the exhaustion from striving sometimes sneak up on us, and we find that we really aren't satisfied with our lives. If we have gained some wisdom, we do not look to blame others for the predicament in which we find ourselves. Instead, we look at what is going on within us.

Turning attention inward allows us to see where we are hooked and what habits contribute to being hooked. We are able to gain insight simply being with the experience of those moments without reacting to them. It allows us to see past our preconceptions and instead interact with what is behind our habits. In this way, we learn how to live in a peaceful and joyful way rather than with strife and unhappiness or maybe even downright misery. In fact, we may find the desire to go beyond the cycle of dissatisfaction. No one likes to feel miserable; we all want to be happy. I've heard this statement many times from various sources, so I conducted a survey with those within my meditation community. It was an anonymous survey of sorts. After their eyes were closed, I asked each of them to raise their right hand and hold their fingers in fist. I then asked everyone who wanted to be happy to raise one finger. Guess what? They all raised a finger. Thankfully, they were all very polite and raised their index finger, and not one of them chose unhappiness over happiness. It was a small sample, but I think we can safely say that everyone wants to be happy.

The American dream of working hard and finding success is part of our conditioning. As we grow up we are conditioned, either overtly or covertly, into accepting the premise of our culture. In fact, this mentality goes well beyond the borders of the United States; we can see this conditioning in many places. We have come to believe that if we are able to fulfill this dream, we will be happy and live a meaningful life. The 1950's in America was a time of hard work and material gain, and those who have grown up in America since have been influenced by this materialistic culture. Yet we are less happy now with a higher rate of suicide, drug addiction, alcoholism, and mental illness, which seems contradictory to our wealthy, industrialized, and free country.

Although Americans have relatively good lives (most of us have enough food to eat, a roof over our heads, and good health), as a society we are still dissatisfied. Not only are we unhappy, but in our attempts to become happier, we have multiplied our difficulties by seeking happiness outside of ourselves. Buying into materialism, we have sought the gods, not of conventional religion like Catholicism, but other isms like, commercialism, materialism, and alcoholism. We aren't bad people and it is not that material things are bad either; they just don't provide us with what we seek long term. In fact, they can even become an overwhelming burden when we have to care for them, repair and clean them, or even worse, move them somewhere else. We just don't know how to find happiness and peace without these things.

As a school teacher, I can tell you that we don't place an emphasis in schools on how to live. Generally, we don't teach that happiness is found inside of us. Instead, we place our emphasis on what to get. Get your education, get your diploma, get good grades, and get a job. Once youngsters graduate from high school, society emphasizes: get married, get pregnant, then get the kids out of the house, and have a good retirement full of travel and play, and so it goes. During our lifetime, we often aren't lucky enough to find even a single person to tell us to stop trying to get something and sit down and rest.

I was fortunate enough to stumble upon such a person several years ago, and that chance encounter changed my life. It was like one of those moments you see in a movie when the clouds slightly part and rays of light shine down upon the earth, and you just know something wonderful is going to happen. The clouds, in this case, weren't the ones in the sky; instead, they were the ones in my own mind that had obscured my joy and happiness for as long as I can remember. During my first meditation retreat, it felt like I was coming home, not to my parents' house, but back to myself. It was an experience without equal. I know this sounds pretty fanciful, but how can anyone adequately explain the beauty of the experience of sitting on the beach and watching the sun set, or the taste of cheesecake with strawberries on top, or how it feels to hold your newborn baby? Maybe poets come closest to being able to describe such things, but they are still light years away from the description of a moment of insight, a dropping away of the veil that blinds us to the truth of this perfect moment. Even if I could describe this experience perfectly, the small (confused) mind would have a tendency to distort it and misunderstand even the description. It is not until we experience this *coming home* for ourselves that we truly understand, that we really *know* the experience. Already I have made this sound mystical (you see how tricky language is). However, the experience of coming back to ourselves is not mystical as much as it is transformative and liberating.

Even though our strategy for happiness is fraught with pitfalls, we keep doing the same thing, and when it doesn't work, we work at it harder. If we do gain some status, comfort, and wealth, we quickly find we want more. The more we get the more we want and the more we have the more we have to work to keep it. Life becomes a struggle as we try to capture the big prize—Success! Yet, what is it that we long for at the end of our lives? When we have all the material things in life, are we left sorrowful that we can't take them with us? Do we feel we missed out on our lives? Or do we feel ready to let go of this life? In the end, do we wish we could have purchased a new BMW? Those who work with the dying don't often hear these kinds of regrets. Instead, they hear people express the sentiment that they wish they had been happier, less worried about everything, less angry, and filled with more appreciation for their lives.

It seems we get accustomed to the struggle. It creeps up on us slowly, and we may not even realize there is a way to go beyond it. Maybe we become complacent because we see everyone else around us doing the same thing, so it must be the "right" thing to do. We don't notice our predicament until it is too late.

There is wisdom within each of us that knows the nature of reality. It is innate; all we need to do is uncover it.

Liberation may sound like a grandiose idea but only if you look at it from a conditioned perspective, which is based on what has been learned from parents, friends, family, and, more generally, culture. This misinformation about the nature of experience has been passed down through a long lineage of misunderstanding from one person to another and within societies. Thus, delusion arises, based on ignorance of the truth of the way things are. We think we see clearly, but it is only when we examine ourselves closely that we begin to see the story of our dissatisfaction unravel.

When life is seen through the eyes of wisdom, we discover that we are the creators of our angst, and we want nothing more than to live a life of freedom. We become like a person who has gone without water for days and sets out in search of a cooling drink. Every ounce of energy is directed towards getting water. Nothing can distract the person from the search for relief. Like this, liberation brings relief. All our pursuits and efforts directed towards material success are a misdirected search based on a misunderstanding and a great deal of conditioning, leading us away from the quenching drink of freedom from confusion and into the desert of striving, loneliness, sorrow, anger, and hatred. Our thirst can be quenched by coming back home to our essence, the ineffable "being-ness" itself.

Let's gently hold the idea, at least for a little while, that we can completely go beyond our conditioning and free ourselves. In this way, we have already cultivated an open heart that allows for this possibility. There is good evidence that this is completely possible. There are ordinary people who, in even the most difficult circumstances, have been able to go beyond their conditioned and painful perspectives. Although we call these people extraordinary now, it was only by what they finally accomplished that this title was bestowed upon them. Up until that point, they were ordinary people like you and me.

The information I am sharing comes from a lineage of people who put meditation practices as taught by the Buddha and other great masters into their everyday lives. Meditation practices have a 2,500-year proving period. It is not new age or even religious wisdom; it is practical yet enlightened wisdom. There are many forms of meditation practice, including sitting meditation, walking meditation, prayer, mantra, dance, and visualization. They all work to help us stay in awareness as much as possible, so we know what is going on within us and aren't living our lives partially and unconsciously. Through meditation and taming our wild minds, we become conscious; we become a complete human being living a full life.

Sometimes this wisdom seems counterintuitive, but this is only because we are not familiar with what is really happening. We don't really understand how things exist, mostly because we haven't been taught or investigated for ourselves. This wisdom is an antidote to uninformed views and strong habit energy. In some parts of our lives, it will seem as though we have the Grand Canyon of habit energy, as if a deep gorge has been carved into our consciousness that seems incapable of being changed. However, this is just more habit energy trying to dissuade us from moving forward in our lives.

It is sometimes uncomfortable to move out of our routines and habits and be exposed to new ideas and new ways of interacting with our lives. Although there is a pull to gain some peace of mind and mental well-being, there are often many concerns expressed by those who are new to looking inward. Habit energy pulls us back into our comfort zone, making it extremely easy to dismiss change. We all have some familiarity with this since many of us have tried to increase exercise programs, decrease the consumption of sweets, stop drinking, smoking, complaining, or overspending. It isn't long before we are back in our rut doing the same thing we committed to changing just a week prior. With some diligence, effort, and patience, we are able to see in new ways and experience the world with new eyes. Our lives become meaningful as we gain insight into the nature of life itself, and we will become free.

My hope is you will take what I share with you and try it on for yourself. It is not enough to hold these new ideas up in front of you like a woman in a department store who doesn't want to make the effort of trying on new clothes. For change to take place, effort is needed to try out what is learned, removing what is old and trying on something new. When we undress from our conditioned mind, we will find a deeper and more profound way to see the world. With openheartedness and a willing attitude, we can transform our ingrained habits and avoid getting lulled into staying in a pot of dissatisfaction. If we are openhearted and willing, we are sure to benefit and transform our dissatisfaction into peace and something much deeper than even joy.

2

A Rare and Precious Opportunity

What a rare and precious opportunity to be born a human being and to have survived until this moment to even speak about this extraordinary freedom. Not only have we been born human, but we also have intelligence and leisure. It is helpful to reflect on how to use this great fortune. Do we only want to eke out a living and entertain ourselves? Is this enough to make our lives meaningful? Are we really living or are we waiting to live? Many realize in the end that they have directed their efforts towards meaningless pursuits and regret they weren't able to live a life filled with more joy. Developing an appreciation for our lives, no matter what is happening, helps us to live with joy rather than with clenched fists and knotted stomachs. It is good to remind ourselves of how precious each moment is and then to live them all fully.

It is very rare to be born a human being, although there seem to be way too many people in the world. In relation to other mammals and species, humans are a small minority. There are approximately 5,490 identified mammals in the world, human beings being one of them. Worldwide, there are an estimated 1,000,000 different insect species, making up about 57 percent of the known species.[5] I don't even want to mention the immense and various species of cockroaches. Okay, I can't help myself: there are 4,000 different species of cockroaches.[6] Maybe you can begin to see that it is indeed quite rare to be born a human being. Somehow, we have made it through year after year without the flame of our lives being extinguished. Yet at any moment, between this breath and the next, we can die. There is no guarantee of even one more inhalation. Even rarer than being born as a human, is being born as a human and meeting with these liberating teachings that shine a light on how to live life in a manner that brings joy to ourselves and others rather than acrimony.

There are many places in the world where these teachings have not yet been shared. Even if they are available in our local community, we may never hear of them. It may take years or even lifetimes to run across this profound wisdom. In other words, these teachings are very profound, and anyone who has the chance to hear them is fortunate. However, it will take some effort to put the wisdom of these teachings into our everyday lives. As with any habit, it will take some effort to transform them.

Each winter, an inversion layer rests just above the valley floor in Boise. It traps the cold air, the city takes on a gray hue, and temperatures plummet, often staying below zero for days and sometimes weeks. Bereft of the blue sky and bright sun, it is easy to become depressed or weary in the midst of the inversion's hold on the city and its inhabitants. It seems it will never end. Yet, with just a short drive to higher ground, one can rise above the cloud layer and into the clear, brilliant light of the sun and blue sky. Like this, we can put forth effort to go beyond the inversion of our minds and into the light of joy. In this way, we take full advantage of this valuable human life.

Having the fortune of this life is like discovering an island full of precious gems. We certainly don't want to come back empty-handed. There is a metaphor in the Sutras that describes the improbability of being born a human. It is so rare, it is akin to a blind turtle swimming in the vast ocean that pops his head up every hundred thousand years, and upon rising to the surface, finds he has stuck his head through a yoke that has been floating atop the same ocean. The chances of this happening, as said by the Buddha, are improbable.

We have this human life, and the most useful and meaningful task we can accomplish is to expand our hearts and go beyond limiting concepts and actions that we have been conditioned into and live our lives with deeper motivations that have an enduring impact on our lives and on others. In essence, our lives can become more fully lived.

When I have met with people to discuss their spiritual journey, several have expressed a feeling that there is something bigger for them in this life, something that will make life meaningful. Unfortunately, this gets translated solely into mundane pursuits as their focus is placed on a career as the thing that will make life meaningful. For example, one young man told me that he has this feeling that there is something bigger waiting for him in this life. I became very excited to hear this because I thought we were going to have a conversation about his meditation practice and his desire to look more deeply into himself. Instead, he said, "I don't like my job, and I know there is a better job for me, something that will be meaningful." There may indeed be a better job out there. It may even involve higher pay, but finding this is not the most meaningful thing he can do.

Finally, deciding on the perfect career or working extra hard to make a lot of money will not bring ultimate freedom, nor will quitting a job and wandering about the world bring this freedom. Instead of thinking of life in a mundane manner, we can place a higher value on it. We can be free as the Buddha became free. Siddhartha Gautama, the Buddha's name prior to enlightenment, didn't focus his attention on the mundane things in life. He could have put all of his efforts into building his father's empire. His time could have been spent in an office, or he could have stayed inside the palace walls and been waited on by beautiful women, but this was not how he decided to spend his time. Instead, he placed all of his efforts towards awakening, meditating, and contemplating to attain the highest realization. Thus, he became known as the Awakened One.

Fortunately, each of us has all we need to be liberated, just as the Buddha did; it is our inborn nature. We can uncover it, and even if we only glimpse it, we will find even greater motivation to continue to see into our true nature. Our lives, just as they are, will provide us with many opportunities to delve deeper into our inner world, to clear away the veil that keeps us from seeing our true face. We don't need to go off into the mountains and away from the world (although this is nice to do every now and again, as it can really help us to uncover hidden aspects of ourselves). There are plenty of opportunities to live in awareness at home, in our workplace, and in relationship with others.

We often take our lives for granted, and out of our ignorance we delude ourselves about impermanence, thinking that because we are alive now, we will also be alive tomorrow. Periodically, however, we may get a wake-up call that stuns us into the realization that our future is not guaranteed. Yet, all too soon we may sink back into delusion again by believing this body to be lasting, when it is impermanent. We only have to sit with the dead for a short time to realize the body is like a log. After some time, we don't even want to come near a corpse, even if it is the body of a loved one we held so dear.

When we stop deluding ourselves about the impermanence of life, we will then establish a strong motivation to change. We can remember not to take this life for granted and to use the time we have to transform our lives, not because we should, but because we can take this pathway to joy, even liberation, and be of benefit to others. Otherwise, we may stay caught up in life's complications and miss realizing what a great gift we have in our possession, pristine Buddha Nature, an already enlightened nature, and instead behave as though we are in some way lacking. Although we already have the perfect jewel of Buddha Nature, we go out into the world looking for fulfillment when it is within us, waiting for us to see it and celebrate it. As an antidote to forgetfulness, upon waking each morning we can wipe our brow and exclaim, "Yes! I woke up. I'm still alive!" Cultivating this kind of gratefulness brings about appreciation and a drive to live in a meaningful way, to wake up from the dream of our uninvestigated mind and into the fullness of our being. It really is a miracle to wake each morning. Like a candle set outdoors, the slightest breeze can extinguish it. Yet here we are, living another day.

Nature is a good reminder of impermanence. The seasons change from spring to summer, fall to winter. Everything is always changing. From the birth and death of stars to the cells in our bodies, every moment is different. Aren't we surprised when we periodically look in the mirror and see our aging face? It is as if gravity increased overnight, and our face shows the result. That smooth, unlined smile we had in our youth now looks like a shriveled apple that's been left in the sun too long. Not seeing this change as it is happening is a result of relating to a habituated mind. We feel we are still twenty-five even when we are in our fifties, or is this just me? It seems that overnight, a new wrinkle emerges, and my small mind can't relate to these changes. The habituated mind is inflexible and static; it doesn't relate to the changes that are occurring moment by moment. The Greek philosopher, Heraclitus, who lived between 544–483 BC, pointed out, "No man ever steps in the same river twice, because it is never the same river and he's not the same man."[7] We are always changing. Even in this very moment changes are occurring around and within us. For example, in the time it takes to read this sentence, billions of changes have occurred in the cells of your body.

Recently, a friend of mine became very concerned when she learned her house was built on a large fault line. It is predicted that there will be a major earthquake along this particular fault line soon. Jokingly, she entertained a small group of us with her dramatic explanation about how her house can go from the top of the hill, where it is currently perched, to the deep valley below when this earthquake hits. We all had a good laugh at her dramatic telling of this possible scenario. In truth, we are always subject to this shaky ground, regardless of the terrain under our feet. There is no solid ground for us to stand on because everything is always changing.

A few years ago my daughter and I were driving down the road, laughing and visiting with one another when a duck landed right in front of the car ahead of us. A second didn't even pass before the car ran over the neck of the duck. There wasn't a thing the driver could have done, nor was there anything my daughter and I could do but witness this event. The duck landed and it died in an instant. Immediately the duck's mate landed next to it and sat there surveying the scene. My daughter and I immediately gasped, and a sense of stunned silence enveloped us as tears pooled in our eyes. We didn't have a chance to turn away, and it became a blessing for both of us because it imbedded a deep appreciation for our lives and the utter fragility of this human existence. We both bring this up to each other every once in a while to remind us of how very fortunate we are to have this human life.

This talk of the possibility of dying may initially sound morbid or depressing. However, when we have a strong sense of the preciousness of this life and the rare opportunity we have been given, we will end up living in a way that isn't obstructed by fear, worry, and hatred. Instead, accepting the impermanent nature of everything frees us from the discomfort of clinging. We can't control life, and the sooner we gain a deep realization of this, the sooner we are freed from the grip of fear.

Accepting the changing nature of everything brings joy, while holding on, being attached, keeps us in the cycle of hope and fear. Objectifying everything and making it solid feels like a monster is lurking around every corner, waiting to take something away from us, whereas truly knowing that the nature of everything is change brings about acceptance and freedom. It is the truth of the way things are so there is no need to cling. Indeed, it is impossible to hold on to anything. Instead, we can see impermanence as divine. When we have attained this immutable view, we can flow with the stream of change and aren't surprised by the rapids or eddies arising in the stream of life. Letting go of attachment is letting go of resistance. We can learn how to let go by meditating on the impermanent nature of our own human form, as well as the impermanence of all circumstances and of all of our friends and family members.

Recently, a student of mine was extremely sad about the loss of her boyfriend. Although he didn't die, she expressed that her future with him did. All of her fantasies about what they would do together in the future were immediately destroyed when he packed up his car and left. She mentioned how hard this was for her to come to grips with and how much sadness this brought her. We tend to live inside these stories of the future; they become real to us, so when we lose them, they cause us much sorrow. In truth, however, they are only stories, fantasies about the future without any solidity or reality. This idea of permanence is a concept. It is simply a mind phenomenon, a thought. In fact, I heard not long ago this same lovely lady has a new boyfriend. Therefore, her projection into the future was a hindrance to her happiness. Understanding the impermanent nature of everything keeps us from taking our lives for granted and allows us to move with the flow of life rather than trying to dam it up, which, of course, is an impossible task anyhow.

Remembering that every action we take has a result, meaning that whatever we do will have an effect, provides fuel for our daily life. We can remind ourselves that whatever seeds we plant will eventually bear fruit. When a watermelon seed is planted, a watermelon grows. We will not go out to the garden one day and find a pine tree where a watermelon was planted. If virtuous seeds are planted, the result will be a virtuous life. Whatever actions we take in life will result in the kind of life we live. There is no separation between an action and its result; they are bound to each other like two sides of the same coin. Therefore, it is helpful to contemplate and investigate our intentions, motivations, hidden agendas, and get clear about what we are doing to make sure we aren't creating unnecessary complications for ourselves and others. Meditation, contemplation, and inquiry enhance our lives so they become richer and more meaningful.

Because everything in this world is temporary in its nature, it always feels as though we are losing something. Often, just when we feel life is almost perfect, tragedy strikes and we fall into despair. The world is full of dramatic, mundane, and disappointing moments. Yes, there are also beautiful moments of new love, babies, a hike in the woods, and a rainbow in the sky. The problem isn't being denied the experience of beautiful moments. The problem is our grasping an idea about life that is incongruent with life itself. We think, *I want this. I don't want that!* Whenever we get what we don't want, we become unhappy, and when we get what we do want, we try to hold onto it. The aversion to difficult moments and clinging to the good moments are the source of our dissatisfaction. Living our lives in this way will not bring the happiness we seek. Instead, it is through letting go of these perspectives that we are able to finally find joy in our lives.

Consider the rare and precious opportunity of meeting with this life, being born a human being with all the freedoms and advantages that we have. Knowing that this life is like a flash of lightening, how will you proceed? The opportunity is in each of our hands—no one else can live our lives for us. In each moment we have the choice. Knowing this, we determine how we will we use this human life. So, if you feel like my student who thinks there is something bigger for him to achieve in this life you are right—there is! It's inner freedom, extraordinary freedom.

It would be a waste to not explore the entirety of our humanness and miss out on the treasure buried within each of us. We can employ awareness and contemplation as skillful means to work with our minds. In order to take full advantage of this life, we become explorers of a previously unexplored dimension, ourselves, and through this we also learn about and appreciate others. Maybe we will find our lives take on new value and meaning.

3

Freedom from the Jail of Thoughts

Most of us are locked in a strange and invisible jail that follows us around. In order to understand what incarcerates us, we must spend time investigating the nature of the jail. This jail is not made up of iron topped with barbed wire and then wrapped with an electrified fence, but it often feels as impenetrable. It is not concrete in any way, yet it appears to be solid and real. Even though we have employed many different strategies, we can't seem to escape. If this jail is not made up of iron or concrete, than what is it made of and how can we penetrate it? If we want to escape, understanding the makeup of these bars will help us employ the right tools to cut through the restraints that keep us from freedom.

When we look at the outer world, we may believe that others chain us and are the source of all of our problems. Perhaps it is our neighbor, politicians, boss, newsmen, cashiers, bad drivers, husband/wife, boyfriend/girlfriend, or a combination of all of the above that is the source of our troubles. If we could only escape from them, we would be okay. We could move to the woods away from society, away from all of our burdens, away from others. However, we find even though we are all alone, there is still a sense of dissatisfaction. The jail still seems to be firmly established, and we continue to feel imprisoned. It logically follows that our imprisonment isn't dependent on others. It must have another source.

Could it be where we live? Maybe our house is too small, or too big, too old, too rundown, and our neighborhood is not good. If we moved it would be better. Our environment is somehow contributing to this entrapment, and we could be happy if we lived in a simpler place, a prettier spot, or a more holy place. We find it doesn't take long for discontent to resurface no matter where we live or the size of our house. If other people and where we live aren't the problem, we may consider looking inward to see if the bars reside inside of us.

We have a plethora of thoughts coming and going. There are thoughts of what we had for breakfast, what we are going to do with our day, thoughts of the past and of the future, good thoughts and bad thoughts, crazy thoughts, scary thoughts, even thoughts about other thoughts. It is hard to concentrate before we are caught up and end up somewhere else. When we investigate by looking into the mind itself, we see that there is nothing solid and concrete; instead, it all seems ephemeral and transient.

By believing thoughts to be "real," we become bound in a jail of thoughts based on a mistaken notion. Thoughts have no realness to them, in that they arise from causes and conditions and are transient, not lasting for more than a moment before another thought forms. So it goes moment after moment, day after day, year after year, until we are lulled into believing that they are real, that they belong to us, and that they can imprison us. Wherever we go, we continually try to think our way out of this cell.

From our thoughts, we establish beliefs and habits. Because most people don't know they are caught behind the bars of their thoughts, they may never consider finding a way to escape. They feel stuck, spinning through life from one crisis to another always searching for a way to feel better, trying to relieve the stagnant discomfort that accompanies them day after day. Trying numerous ways to distract themselves from their dissatisfaction, they inadvertently perpetuate additional dissatisfaction, resulting in sturdier bars. Like flies caught in a spider's web, they are further ensnared with each attempt to escape. They try to grasp onto happiness, solidify what is ephemeral, and reject what is nonexistent. With fierce determination, they fight with the ghosts of their minds (their thoughts), trying to disentangle themselves from the web of confusion.

The problem is not with any individual thought, but with the confidence that the thought is *real* and that we must react or follow or fret about that thought. When we look into the mind and see only thoughts and believe in them, we are ignorant of the basis of thought itself. We don't really know the cause of our dissatisfaction and how to go beyond it. Thankfully, we can take guidance from those who have already walked this path and find our way out of the bars that hold us.

The Buddha discovered the basis of our suffering is ignorance, a lack of understanding about the way things exist. We think that we and phenomena exist solidly and independently, yet this is not the case. We don't understand the nature of reality; instead, we have an idea about reality based on misconception and socially conditioned habits.

As Ludwig Wittgenstein, a philosopher, referenced, "A man will be imprisoned in a room with a door that's unlocked and opens inwards; as long as it does not occur to him to pull rather than push."[8] Our approach to life is based on conditioning and the resulting habits. When life doesn't follow these conditions or if we are entrenched in our habits, we can end up pushing on a door several times before thinking to pull. I'm sure you've seen someone try a door several times before it occurs to them to stop pushing and pull instead. Some people never get it and give up, turning away from the door because the possibility of pulling never arises in their minds. Like this, we are conditioned into the idea of reality as something independent and substantial.

When we inquire into where thoughts come from, we are not able to find a place, nor are we able to find where they go. If we look closely, we find that both "good" thoughts and "bad" thoughts arise and then they cease. They do not come from somewhere nor do they go anywhere. If we continue looking, we find they are insubstantial: they are not solid, they aren't real, and they don't last. In fact, everything is interconnected, arising in dependence on something else appearing to us as separate, but in truth everything has never been apart from "suchness." Suchness, is the groundless ground in which all appears.

Thoughts, like waves appearing on the surface of the ocean, are not separate from the ocean itself. Both are water, yet waves appear. Although thoughts appear, they are not truly existent nor are they separate from the essential luminosity, suchness itself. When we see thoughts are insubstantial, we no longer buy into their content. Just as clouds in the sky change shape and move across the vast expanse of the sky, we can view our thoughts as changing shape, sometimes appearing as harmless, other times appearing as dark and ominous. In either case, they are insubstantial and arise based on causes and conditions and will dissipate when the cause and conditions for their arising no longer exist. Through insight, we gain realization of the nonduality of thoughts and the basic luminous nature of the mind. In other words, thoughts are appearances that have never been separate from awareness itself. So there is no need to engage in an all-out war with our thoughts or to hold onto them as real and be emotionally dragged around by them. Instead, we can see their intrinsic empty nature and watch their arising and ceasing as the display of suchness. In this way, we are unaffected by the play of the mind. Seeing its essential nature, we are freed from the push and pull of our thoughts and instead can abide in the natural state of the mind.

We have been encouraged to experiment for ourselves, not to take these teachings as a belief or a philosophy but to test them out in the lab of personal experience. Think back to a time that a "significant" thought arose and you believed it wholeheartedly, yet it turned out to be completely wrong. An example of such a thought in traditional Buddhist literature is mistaking a rope for a snake. At first glance, we may see a snake on our path and recoil from it, but with further analysis we realize that although the rope appeared to be a snake and we reacted to it as such, it never was a snake. Like this, we look at our thoughts, thinking they are real, but we are mistaken because they have no weight, color, shape, nor substantiality. Like the vapors that take the form of clouds, we don't know where they go when they dissolve. In the same way, when we look at thoughts, they also dissolve. We can't say where a thought goes. We just know when it is no longer there.

We can test this to see if this is true and gain the experience of knowing for ourselves. If we don't see it for ourselves, experience it fully, we won't gain the full benefit. Instead, we will end up with just another belief. For example, would it be more satisfying for me to tell you about the delicious taste of cheesecake or share a piece with you so you can experience its smooth, creamy, deliciousness? If you ate the cheesecake, you would know cheesecake intimately.

In the same way, if we stop and take time to look into our minds, we may find the taste of freedom. Carrying around the *idea* of freedom will never satisfy us. Within our minds are movement, transience, and insubstantiality. There is no solidity to our thoughts. Like a rainbow, they come and go, appearing and disappearing, having no concreteness. Even though they sometimes seem real, when we approach them with awareness we see how silly it is to believe in them as real.

As a child, I grew up believing in Santa Claus. Actually, it was more than a belief; I was deeply in love with Santa. One Christmas Eve, my grandfather took my brother and me out on a drive in search of Santa and his reindeer. We drove around the hills, looking into the night sky, searching for the red nose of Rudolph. Fortunately, my grandfather found Rudolph way up in the sky, and we were able to follow his movements for a little while. My brother and I were so thrilled. When we arrived back home, just missing Santa by moments, presents were piled around the Christmas tree. Ah, what a glorious person Santa Claus was to me.

Maybe you believed in Santa Claus like I did. My belief in Santa was based on a number of thoughts that culminated in a belief. Even when there was very strong evidence that Santa didn't exist (my sister's friends all told me he wasn't real), I convinced myself that he did indeed exist, as well as the Easter Bunny and the Tooth Fairy. I still vividly remember the moment when I was told the horrible news that Santa was not real. I was sitting at the kitchen table, and I asked my dad if what my sister and her friends had been telling me were true. "Is there really no Santa Claus?" He confirmed my inquiry with "No, there is no Santa Claus." It truly broke my heart. I had invested so much into believing in him that it was hard to let go. As I sat in stunned disbelief, it occurred to me that the Tooth Fairy and the Easter Bunny may also be unreal. Once I received confirmation, I never thought of them as real again.

In the same way that Santa Claus was held as an elaborate belief, a set of thoughts that was never true in the first place, we hold beliefs about the realness of many other thoughts that are so ingrained in us that they are difficult to let go. We can remind ourselves that our thoughts never substantially come into being nor go out of being. In fact, this is the case for everything. In my example, it was not as though Santa Claus was real and then he became unreal—there was never an ounce of realness to Santa Claus from the beginning. When we see our thoughts like this, we are no longer tied to their whims. They can no longer drag us around.

Let's not make the mistake of replacing our ordinary thoughts with spiritual thoughts, thinking this is a means of escape. Of course it is very nice to have spiritual thoughts. It makes our life look more pleasant, as well as making the experiences of those around us seem more pleasant. There is nothing like hanging around a grouchy person for a while to gain an appreciation for people with more pleasant dispositions. However, being attached to pleasant thoughts still binds us. When these turn to painful ones, we long for the return of pleasant thoughts.

Life and thoughts are made up of many textures; to pick one over all others is bound to cause unhappiness. In addition, simply taking on spiritual thoughts, like spiritual clothing, doesn't free us. True insight into the nature of thought is what is required in order to be free. True insight provides the doorway to freedom out of the jail of thoughts. Even though it was painful to hear that Santa Claus didn't exist, it was also freeing because I didn't have to keep trying to convince myself of his realness. Like this, there is freedom in realizing our thoughts are unreal, have never been real, and our belief in them has bound us to suffering.

Looking at thoughts in this way, we see their ultimate nature, which is empty of any inherent existence. It is said that the Buddha inquired into the nature of thought by asking, "Where is thought?" He pointed out that, when looking for thought, it can never be seen or even apprehended. It is like a magical illusion, for with imagination it colors the world. We react to the world with distorted lenses, thinking things are real when they aren't. Sometimes we paint the world with beautiful thoughts and at other times with dark and foreboding thoughts, both of which are from our imagination. We miss the opportunity to experience the clarity of the ultimate by getting caught up with what's passing in front of our awareness, instead of letting it come into existence and go out of existence as it does by itself. Instead, we analyze it, grab hold of it, try to manipulate it, and then engage with the abstract concept about life rather than life itself.

If we realize our folly, we become like someone who has been incarcerated for years and is finally freed. Thoughts no longer have the power to keep us chained; even very powerful thoughts don't possess inherent power to lock us within their prison. Rather than perpetuating the habit of viewing thoughts as solid entities full of important content, we can see a new way to interact with them, see them as the display of suchness itself. Accordingly, Buddha pointed out that all material and mental structures manifest as one continuous presence, one absolute depth of unthinkable purity, without any trace of positive or negative assertion.[9] In other words, all phenomena and thoughts, concepts, and beliefs, are manifestations of suchness—pure, pristine, and luminous—without any notion of positive or negative. When this truth is seen, there are no dualistic notions of positive and negative. Things are seen as they are. With this new insight, we will not be bound to the jail of our thoughts. In fact, we find that there was never a jail in the first place; the thought of a jail holding us is simply another thought. We can let go of our struggle with our thoughts and see them as a divine display of awareness.

4

Healing the Cancer
of Delusion

When we were young, around the time we could still stick our toes in our mouths, we had the freedom to just be. It was okay to suck on our toes at that time. It was okay until someone told us it wasn't. Over the years as we've been conditioned, we've learned belief systems, the rules of our culture, and other rules that have impinged on our freedom. In a lot of ways, this is very good: everyone walks around in clothes; most people stop when the light turns red and go when the light turns green. We abide by rules that work for society. However, on top of this, we have layered beliefs and concepts considered inherent to being human that are not benefiting us.

Crystallized concepts and beliefs are like a cancer that veils our true nature. This cancer is the cancer of delusion, and it is based on ignorance and unfamiliarity with our true nature. It creates the belief in self and others, and because of this belief, we become caught in ignorance. We are unaware of a way to escape. Indeed, some people are not even aware they are caught. As a result, mental angst is pervasive. Due to the strength of our habit energy and the lack of insight into the basis of our dissatisfaction, life becomes a struggle. It seems to be a part of the human condition; however, it is possible to see through all concepts and beliefs and unveil the truth.

The Buddha noted that the Dharma is the medicine to relieve our suffering, and he is like a physician who prescribes the medicine. What he didn't say is that he would prescribe the medicine, fill the prescription, and then administer it. If we are suffering and we want to go beyond it, then we will need to take the medicine ourselves.

People who are diagnosed with cancer often go through all sorts of uncomfortable, frightening, and painful procedures. Because they want to live, they are often willing to do whatever it takes. You may have family members who have cancer or perhaps you have experienced cancer. Cancer patients have to endure uncomfortable and painful procedures for the possibility of a cure. They are probed and prodded by a physician, blood is drawn, and sometimes a painful bone marrow biopsy is performed. If the tests come back indicating cancer in the body, the patient will be given a prescription for fighting the cancer: chemotherapy and/or radiation treatment to destroy the cancer cells. During the course of the treatment, hair may fall out and the patient may become extremely ill, experience weight loss, and loss of appetite. But because the patient wants to live, there is a strong motivation and a willingness to endure all the discomforts of the treatment.

Like the cancer patient, we, too, are overtaken by cancer—the cancer of delusion. In order to be free from this delusion, we will need to take the medicine, the Dharma, and have the same strong motivation to be willing to do whatever it takes to free ourselves from the cycle of sorrow.

Because the pull of our habits is so strong, it may be hard to accept the medicine. The medicine tastes sweet to some and is difficult to swallow for others. The tug of our habits pulls us so strongly that sometimes it is uncomfortable to make a change. However, with a strong motivation, we are able to follow through and take the medicine.

Sometimes this motivation comes about because we hit rock bottom, we can't stand our situation any longer, or we become sick and tired of being sick and tired. We become disgusted. This is a great motivator and a great gift because there is nothing else we can do. Everything we have been doing has not been working. Our mate hasn't made it better; eating, drinking, shopping, and vacations have not made our lives better. Of course, I'm not saying that there aren't some good moments, but for many people there are very few. At this point, all resources are used up and nothing in this world seems to help. We become willing to take the medicine. For some, it really is a fight for life. They may be on the brink of giving up on life, and through some wonderful synchronicity, they hear the Dharma and are willing to follow the prescription as outlined.

When we find that nothing is satisfying, life becomes meaningless. I knew someone who used to periodically drink distilled water as a means to cleanse her liver. I'm not advocating this, but I did drink the distilled water when I was with her. Distilled water is very unsatisfying. It is as if there is nothing in it. It is very strange. It is wet, it looks like water, but when you drink it you can sense there is something missing. Like this, many people feel there is something missing in this life, so a spiritual search begins.

We can call it a spiritual journey with the hope of finding a satisfying life. We are seeking something, yet we don't even know what. In Buddhist terms, we might say we are seeking realization. This can actually end up being a pitfall on the path, believe it or not, but we have to start somewhere, and we are all in a different place.

We are all on a spiritual path for our own reasons. We may know these reasons and we may not. However, to make a change, we need to fill the prescription. This particular prescription gets filled every day. It is like grocery shopping in Italy: they don't go once a week or once a month. Instead, they go every day and pick up fresh lettuce, fresh tomatoes, and fresh bread and then go home and make a meal. Like this, we sit in meditation every day and with insight our view changes. We change the way we see the world. Everywhere we go becomes a paradise. Rather than experience being something to either grasp or avoid, every experience we have propels us towards a new way of seeing.

Many of our habits are based in fear. We want to control life, to secure it, so we grasp at clear blue sky, moderate temperatures, money in the bank, and peace, to name a few. We have an aversion towards freezing temperatures, illness, and a lack of any kind. We have been spending our lives like a ping-pong ball, going back and forth between grasping and aversion. This is what creates the sense of becoming sick and tired of being sick and tired. We exert a lot of effort towards worrying, seeking after an unachievable goal. Like a hamster trying to get somewhere while running on its wheel within a cage, we chase after something that we can never achieve. Each goal either advances as we move towards it, or as soon as we achieve a goal, we create a new one.

This doesn't mean we give up everything or stop setting goals. We can have everything we currently have, and we don't even have to clean out the junk drawer. It is not about that. It is about changing our view. The prescription is an everyday activity. In order to make true change, it is a moment-by-moment activity. When we meditate, we eventually learn to "be" with whatever appears in our mind stream regardless of its beauty or ugliness. We learn to live a more uncontrived and aware life.

A while back, someone told me they thought meditation was really difficult. She felt as though she was going to explode. We all have days where we feel challenged by meditation. We feel that the person in charge of ringing the bell to end the meditation session must not be looking at the time, or maybe is out to get us. Perhaps they aren't focused, because it has to be time for the bell to ring! Maybe you've also had this experience. You sit down to meditate for twenty minutes and you look down at the clock, thinking twenty minutes have passed, and it has only been five minutes.

Another person shared with me how difficult meditation was at a retreat she attended. She was tortured by her mind and belief in her thoughts. During her meditation she kept thinking, *How can I get out of this retreat?* Unfortunately, the retreat was in a remote area, so to get out of it would have been difficult. Not only was it in a remote area, but it was the middle of winter where the temperature sometimes dipped down to minus twenty degrees.

I have a backpack, so I can walk out of here. That would work. Then she realized she came with someone else. Even if she did get out to the road, she wouldn't be able to drive away.

I can call a taxi. I'll call them before I hike out and then they can pick me up and take me to the closest town. Great! But what do I do when I get to the closest town? The airport is hours away.

She went through all of these possibilities during her meditation, sitting at 6:30 a.m., 9:00 a.m., 10:00 a.m., and 11:00 a.m. She continued in this way, all day long, planning her escape. Finally, during one of the meditation sessions, she got so sick of her mental angst and complex plans to escape that she finally just gave up and let go of all planning. She simply sat with her emotions and let herself feel uncomfortable. Not too much time passed, and she felt complete freedom. Then she thought, *This is the best retreat ever. I'm so happy I'm here. I can't believe how fortunate I am to be able to be in this retreat.* Essentially, there was no escape, there was no back door, and she had no way out. Her only option was to let go.

Our training is about letting go. When thoughts arise, we simply notice they are arising. When we engage with them, like the woman at the retreat engaged with them, we may have a battle on our hands. Through this struggle, we can learn something about ourselves. We learn that when we let go, life becomes easier. When we grasp or cling, it is painful.

I used to practice aikido, which involves working with a partner. The idea is that you work with the empty spaces inherent in an attack. When your partner attacks, you move with their energy, and essentially they make themselves fall. This is a very simplistic explanation (Aikido masters, please excuse this inadequate description). There were a few big men in that class, and they were my favorites. Although my ego wasn't supposed to be involved, it was. I really enjoyed the times I could throw a big man on the ground. That always felt great.

When one resists the attack, the attacker has the advantage. If you think, *I'm going to push this man down and it's going to feel great,* you usually end up on the ground yourself with your partner peering down at you from above suggesting that you try again. You get up, sweaty and exhausted and try again and again until you realize *I can't push this person down*. When aikido is approached without resistance, the attacker falls on his own.

If you've been fighting with life, you might feel like I did in aikido, and you are ready to stop fighting and let life's challenges fall on their own. The army of thoughts is a powerful force. Meditation is not about fighting with the army of thoughts; instead, it is the art of sitting with whatever arises and letting it be.

Meditation brings us back home to our true selves, our true nature. Most of us don't know our true selves because we are afflicted with the cancer of delusion. However, if we change our view and see that we are already endowed with everything, that our nature is untainted and luminous, then we don't have to seek for others to tell us who we are, or seek out experiences that bring attention to ourselves, or feel bad when people say harmful things about us. Instead, we can take everything onto the path of awareness.

This brings us to the place of freedom. We cure the cancer of delusion by seeing the truth that every mundane structure is the lion's roar of perfect wisdom, as is noted in *Mother of the Buddhas*.[10] Meditation can lead us to experience insight, taking us beyond our confused mind and help us to see things as they are—extraordinary. Grains of sand, a snowflake, a dust mote, are all extraordinary. When we look at all of life through the eyes of the unconditioned, we see what an amazing display it is, and the cancer of delusion is transcended.

5

Adversity Is Not
the Problem

I read a story about Alice Herz Sommer who was sent to a
concentration camp in the Czech Republic, along with her
parents, husband and young son. Her parents were killed
immediately, and later her husband was taken to Dachau
where he died. When she and her son were eventually freed
from the concentration camp, she returned to her home to
find it was taken over by others who now lived there. Despite
being incarcerated in a concentration camp, experiencing
the deaths of her husband and parents, and losing her
home, when asked what her secret for feeling so good was,
she mused, life is beautiful.[11] She had learned how to be
thankful for everything. While still knowing there were bad
things, she chose to look at the good in life. Even though
she had experienced much loss and great challenges, she
held no hatred in her heart. She didn't view the adversity
she experienced as a problem.

This woman was subjected to extremely great challenges, but it didn't diminish her ability to see the beauty in life and to be thankful for everything. There are many stories of those who have undergone extreme hardship, and either it didn't diminish their already optimistic view or it enhanced their view and appreciation for life. Through being open, they were able to go beyond ordinary reactions to their challenging circumstances and see them differently.

We can also gain this insight and change the way we respond to challenges. Our challenges may not be as great as those experienced in the atrociousness of a concentration camp, but challenging situations arise in everyone's life. Even the Buddha had challenging situations arise in his life after he became enlightened. At one point, he was shot in the foot by an arrow, and later, facing the ultimate adversity, he was inadvertently poisoned by spoiled food that resulted in his death. He also had troublesome monks and lay people around him who misunderstood his teachings. Some people will have many more challenges than others. However, it is not whether or not we have challenges, but how we deal with these challenges that will determine the kind of life we live.

Many of those who visit with me after I give a Dharma talk come to tell me about their challenges. They share stories of adversities they have faced or are currently facing and ask, *Why me?* When we become ill we ask, *Why am I sick?* When challenging people or situations come into our lives we ask, *Why can't I just have peace?* When we are broke, we ask, *When other people have what they need, why don't I?* These are not unusual questions; you may have also asked similar ones. We pay a lot of attention to these types of conversations we have with ourselves. It is as though we believe that life can be good forever, but then a problem comes along to ruin it all. We might think, *If only one person was nice to me I'd be happy. If only I were rich I would be happy. If only this situation were not a part of my life I'd be happy.*

We spend an extraordinary amount of mental effort trying to get away from what we consider "negative" aspects of life. When life is showering us with blessings, when everything is pleasing to us, we expect it to stay that way. This is so engrained in us that we don't often ask the questions, *Why me? Why did I get such a wonderful partner? Why am I so healthy when other people are unhealthy?* If we are going to ask why we get sick, it is equally valid to wonder why we aren't sick more often or how we have stayed healthy up to this point.

Theodore Isaac Rubin, a noted psychiatrist, said, "The problem is not that there are problems. The problem is expecting otherwise and thinking that having problems is a problem."[12] This is a somewhat radical perspective, isn't it? There is deep wisdom in his statement; if we are able to go beyond the expectation that life should not have challenges, then we will be in alignment with life. We will be able to let go of our struggle with life.

Life is the experience of wholeness; it is only in our minds that it is divided into good and bad or problem and no problem. Once we are able to see this, we are then in line with the flow of life itself. We are no longer trying to avoid half of life. When we accept the wholeness of life by not divvying it up into negative or positive experiences, we are then freed from problems.

If we can't accept this premise as proposed, we can use the advice given by Shantideva, who pointed out that if there is a remedy when trouble strikes, what reason is there for despondency? And if there is no help for it, what use is there in being sad?[13] If there's something that we can do about a problem then do it, but if there's nothing that we can do about it, then why resist? Why be sad? If we can do something, then we don't really have a problem. Although the "doing" may be a challenge, we would not consider it a problem. Once we have done what we can do, what is the point in causing ourselves further misery by resisting what is? If we approach life in this way, we will not experience the roller coaster of strong emotions.

It appears that we are experiencing life directly when we fight against adversity and cheer for peace, but these are illusory, occurring in our mind, unreal in the sense that our reaction to them is based on our perception, not on the experience itself. Instead of dealing with what is really happening, we end up dealing with the story we are creating about the situation. Although it seems that we're seeing reality all the time, what we are actually experiencing is our limited perception, which is strained through the sieve of our past experiences. Since everything is filtered through our mind, it is illusory in nature, like a dream. Even scientists agree.

Neuroscientists Susan Martinez-Conde and Stephen Macknick said in an article in *Scientific American Mind*, "It's a fact of neuroscience that everything we experience is actually a figment of our imagination. Although our sensations feel accurate and truthful, they do not necessarily reproduce the physical reality of the outside world."[14] We are sometimes fooled by what we see because our eyes only give us part of the information out there, then our visual system fills in the missing information with a plausible interpretation based on our background knowledge and our past experiences.

These same scientists share an interesting experiment in their book, *Slights of Mind,* looking into *inattentional blindness.*[15] A ball was passed between two groups of people: a group dressed in white and another dressed in black. The task of the observer was to count how many passes were made between those dressed in white only. In order to tally these passes correctly, the observers needed to have a strong, single-pointed focus on the ball, as well as on the color of the shirt of the person who threw the ball and the one who caught it. Because the observers' focus was so singular, they didn't notice that at some point a bear danced through the scene. Most of the observers totally missed the bear, even though he walked right through the middle of the action.

Buddhist thought goes beyond what the scientific community has observed. We can expand our understanding of the illusory nature of our experience beyond visual input to all of our experiences. Through meditation and insight, the Buddha discovered everything is like a dream. The *Lankavatara Sutra* notes that there is nothing but thought.[16] Like an image in the air, there are no realities anywhere that we can hold on to. Through training the mind, we become capable of seeing into the true nature of reality rather than interacting with our world based on what we *think* is real.

If we view our problems in a different way by seeing their illusory nature, we can go beyond them. Employing different strategies to go beyond our ingrained habits will help us. Because problems are a construct of the mind, we can change the way we view them and use them to liberate us from the sorrow they create. One of the Mind Training slogans, a set of pithy instructions formulated by Geshe Chekewa in the twelfth century, suggests, "When the world is filled with evil, transform all mishaps into the path of Bodhi."[17] (Bodhi means to awaken from confusion.) In relation to our usual view of adversity, this slogan is very radical. To some, it may even seem impossible. Normally, we attempt to run from adversity, but like our shadow, it sticks close to us. This Mind Training slogan instructs us to bring difficulties onto the path, to stay rather than to psychologically run. To bring something onto the path means we use it as a force for changing the way we see the world. Rather than seeing adversity as a detriment, we can see it as a gift that can help us to transform our lives. Using tragedies, imprisonment, or general dissatisfaction as compost for awakening will allow the fullness of our lives to flourish, making our lives more meaningful.

On the other hand, if we fuel adversity with angry and anxious thoughts, it is like adding kindling to a fire. It will only grow stronger, and we won't find peace or happiness. Our normal view is that we'll get burned by the fire of adversity. With such thoughts, it becomes quite scary. We may worry that something bad might happen to us. However, as we walk through adversity, we will start to experience the reality of what's happening in the present moment. Walking into adversity when it presents itself is the act of allowing ourselves to stay with the experience rather than running from it.

I heard a story that illustrates how we can face adversity and find a new perspective on life. This story is about a woman who decided to live life rather than try to hold onto it. She was driving along the freeway in Los Angeles when the traffic in front of her suddenly came to a screeching halt. She slammed on her brakes and stopped just short of hitting the car in front of her. Then, when she glanced in her rearview mirror she realized that the car immediately behind her was still traveling at full speed. With this realization, she let go of the strong grip she had on the steering wheel, closed her eyes, and relaxed. In that moment, she thought to herself that she had always lived her life with a tight grip and decided that this was not how she wanted to live or how she wanted to die. In that same instant the car hit her with all of its force, smashing her car into the car ahead of her. Thankfully, she was able to walk away from the accident, not only with her life, but with a new perspective. By releasing her grip on her idea of how life should be, she found a new way to live. When confronted with adversity, she did what she could do and let life happen. Through taking this approach, she actually saved her life, and it changed the way she interacted with life from that moment forward. Rather than trying to keep a tight grip on life, she was able to let go.

When we sit with adversity, accepting what we cannot change, we will eventually find it disappears on its own. This doesn't mean that we're suddenly cured of cancer or that we get a windfall of money so that our financial situation is now stable. It means we won't consider adversity a problem any longer.

Many stories are told about Nasruddin, an ancient Persian folk character, who appeared to be a fool, but proved again and again that he had a great deal of wisdom. The parable of "Two Questions" involves a local man who approached Nasruddin for advice on how to grow roses. This man had planted rose bushes all around his house, but all that ever grew were dandelions. He asked Nasruddin what he should do in order to get the roses to grow. Nasruddin suggested he use old camel dung to fertilize the roses. But the man had already tried that. Then Nasruddin suggested he grow his roses on the banks of the Tigris River, which the man said would be very inconvenient.

The man then asked, "Do you have any other solutions?"

Nasruddin contemplated this for a while and said, "Yes, but you won't like it."

The man replied, "I will like it."

But Nasruddin continued to hold his tongue, certain the man would not like his solution. Finally the man begged Nasruddin to tell him, saying, "Please, Oh great and wise Nasruddin, please, tell me." The man insisted that Nasruddin share his knowledge in order to solve his problem.

Nasruddin took a deep breath and said, "You must learn to love dandelions."[18]

We can all learn to love dandelions. When we have an open heart full of acceptance, we can accept dandelions when they appear. Of course, it is nice to have beautiful roses, but if they won't grow for us and dandelions will, what is the problem? The only problem is that we don't want what we already have. Learning to accept and appreciate what we have right now will bring us new appreciation for our lives and everything in them. This is a very simple approach yet very difficult at the same time. It's simple in that it's not a multistep program we need to implement. We don't need any special skills; all we need to do is to surrender to what's happening in the moment. This is the simple shortcut. Our paradigm can shift in a way that allows us to see our lives and experiences in a new way, having a profound effect on our lives. Because of our connections to so many other people, this translates into a positive effect on society.

Let me share a couple of true stories about two men who were incarcerated in Chinese labor camps during the Chinese Cultural Revolution. These true stories give me confidence, showing me that I too can transcend my problems and live in a different way, even if my problems are quite severe. His Eminence Garchen Triptrul Rinpoche was incarcerated for twenty years. While imprisoned, his daily job was to make bricks. It was difficult work to do day after day, hour after hour, especially without enough food to sustain him. One fortunate day, he met his heart teacher, someone he had a strong connection with, Khenpo Munsel, who was also incarcerated in the labor camp. As you can imagine, it was an extremely fortunate meeting. Khenpo Munsel gave him instructions on how to do the practice of exchanging oneself for another, called Tonglen, while seeing the nondual nature of suffering. Taking this advice to heart, Garchen Rinpoche changed his perspective; he used all activities in prison as a way to increase love and compassion in his heart.[19]

Gochen Tulku Rinpcohe was incarcerated in a Chinese labor camp for ten years. While incarcerated he had the fortune to meet with many teachers who passed on their wisdom to him. This was quite a challenging time for him. It was during his time of incarceration that his spiritual practice really began. He says, "It was due to the kindness of my masters that I was able to feel compassion instead of hatred toward my captors. No matter how much physical hardship I underwent, my mind felt happy and at ease. This gave me profound confidence in my masters' instructions and the Buddhist teachings."[20] Although he was still in prison, he didn't let a moment pass, he put the teachings he was given into practice in the midst of great hardships. Not only was he able to meet with them but to take them to heart, which allowed him to be liberated inwardly, feeling at ease, prior to being physically released from prison.

Whether we are in prison or not, we have the freedom to do whatever we would like with our minds, but only if we have trained them. Do we want to use our circumstances to free ourselves, or do we want to continue with the same old way of relating to the world? We make this choice in each moment.

As the imprisoned Lama did, we too, can use the Mind Training teaching called Tonglen. We can exchange ourselves for others by putting ourselves in others' shoes through using visualization combined with openheartedness. We visualize taking on the suffering of others and give them love and joy. This doesn't require a new religion or to give up one we may already have. Instead, it is something anyone can do who would like to help themselves and others. It helps us go beyond self-grasping, which causes unhappiness, and opens our heart to others. As a result, we become happier even though that may not have been our intention.

Let me share this practice with you. It has the power to open your heart and relieve your suffering and the suffering of others. Begin this practice by seeing the suffering of all beings as the same as your suffering. Then, meditate on love and compassion for a few moments. As your heart opens, visualize someone you love sitting in front of you. Bring to mind all of the suffering this person has endured and breathe it in as a cloud of black smoke that rises up from your visualized loved one. As it enters your body, your heart expands to the limits of the universe. Then breathe out love in the form of brilliant rays of light that permeate your visualized loved one. Do this for a while, then continue on in this way, repeating the above description, but replace your loved one with yourself visualized sitting across from you. After a while, visualize those you find challenging or consider your enemies, and finally visualize all beings. By spending some time with each of these visualizations, you enhance your ability to experience love and compassion for all beings without preference. With a wish to be of benefit to all beings, you can transform your interactions with others, as well as interactions with yourself.

You can do Tonglen for anyone, anywhere, at any time. It doesn't require a special setting or ritual; it only requires an open heart and the willingness to explore how much further we can open our heart. Any limits placed on opening our hearts are false limits. Our hearts can continually expand, taking in all beings under the umbrella of compassion and loving-kindness.

There is a side benefit to Tonglen. Although we do it to benefit others, we will find that we also benefit from it in profound ways. As our hearts open to others, they are also opening to us. Instead of magnifying our negative habits through judgment, criticism and hatred, as we do with our ordinarily confused minds, with Tonglen, we end up opening our hearts to love, compassion and kindness. These qualities are enhanced while negative qualities are diminished.

It is said that the best way to defeat an enemy is by making the enemy a friend. Tonglen helps us to befriend our fear, lack of control, and desire for things to be different than they are, as well as human enemies. When we are able to loosen our grip on ideas about how things should be and work instead with how things are, we remove the cause of our suffering. The friction caused by the resistance to what is and what we think should be is a cause for misery. When we resist what is in our life in any moment, we develop friction that causes a mental sore, like a rug burn of the mind that causes us pain. Without the mental resistance to the moment, we slide through our experiences, whether positive or negative, with ease. Without resistance, there isn't an idea of a problem, there is only life displaying itself in a myriad of ways.

How we perceive problems not only has an effect on us but it has far-reaching effects, touching all those around us. We can change the world by the way we deal with adversity. If we use it as a path for awakening, we will not be the cause of harm in the world. Instead, we will be a source of peace, understanding, and ease.

6

Tea with My Teachers

Although adversity comes to us unbidden, blindsiding us when we least expect it and sometimes even taking us to our knees, these times in our lives are ripe with the opportunities for getting to know ourselves and changing our relationship to challenges. In fact, adversity can be our greatest teacher; we can meet it at the door with a cup of tea and transform it into the path.

No matter the circumstances we face in our lives, we can use them as a path for freeing ourselves from mental chains. Don't get me wrong—there is no need to go in search of difficulties, nor do we need to invite these circumstances into our lives—they arrive on their own without an invitation. But when adversity does step across the threshold of our lives and plants itself on the couch of our consciousness, we can view it as our teacher and invite it to tea. Kharak Gomchung, a meditation master from the eleventh century, pointed out that, "Difficulties are our spiritual teachers, obstacles are a spur to Dharma practice, and suffering is a broom to sweep away our evil deeds."[21]

In other words, we shouldn't regard difficulties with dislike; instead, we can sit with our experiences of fear, jealousy, humiliation, anxiety, loss, sorrow, and the other myriad emotions that arise when we are confronted with adversity without rejecting them. This does not mean that we wallow in the experience, feeling sorry for ourselves. Nor is this the time to run away and take refuge in something else to relieve the pain. Shopping for shoes, having a cocktail, or turning on the television will only prolong our discomfort; it does not remove it. When we run from negative circumstances, our discomfort lingers in the backgrounds of our lives expressed as stress, discontent, depression, and/or physical ailments. Instead, we can use awareness to see the root of the experience. In this way, we can uproot the whole of our sorrow rather than simply chopping away at its branches.

Although we all prefer positive experiences, they often don't propel us to change the way we view the world as adversity does. When others treat us poorly, we can remember these people as teachers who are challenging our attachment and aversion. In other words, if we are able to stay with whatever we are experiencing in a nonjudgmental manner, our thought, belief, concept, or emotion will transform itself. Through being aware of what is going on in our minds and not judging or reacting to it, we are able to live our lives with more equanimity and peace.

Maybe you've heard the comment that what doesn't kill you makes you stronger. Psychologists are finding this saying to have some merit. Researchers Seery, Holmen, and Silver have found that people who have a history of adversity and are able to overcome it, develop mental resilience as a result, meaning they don't fall apart when life becomes difficult. These people are better able to handle future adversity when it arises.[22]

Unfortunately, our conditioned approach, when challenged by others or by life's circumstances, is to close our hearts. Instead of finding peace, we end up bound to anger, fear, sorrow, and possibly even self-hatred. These experiences place us in the dark forest of tangled emotions. During these times, the ghosts of our thoughts lead us into dark places, and it feels as though we will never find peace. Almost everything in our lives, our upbringing, our societal and cultural rules, our language, and our families and friends, unwittingly support our suffering. We are often consoled by others with words that reaffirm the hopelessness of getting beyond the place we find ourselves. We hear, "Life sucks. What can you do?" Or we may find a lot of support in our negativity directed against those who have caused us harm. Our friends may encourage us to "stick it to him/her" when our husband or wife cheats on us. In fact, we demand such support from our friends and family. No one really likes hearing that it is our mind that is causing the problem. We may even consider this heresy.

This tendency to close ourselves off is like building a wall around our hearts. Sometimes this great wall becomes a seemingly permanent fixture in our consciousness, separating us from love, empathy, compassion, and joy. In a sense, the walls we build around our hearts become a self-created prison. We become filled with fear, hatred, jealousy, and may even end up disconnected from others, resulting in lonely, angry lives. With each hurtful circumstance, the separation between the heart and mind becomes greater. We accumulate resentments and fear, and eventually we are broken by the sheer weight of the baggage we carry.

We often focus on trying to change the situation or person in hopes of finding peace. In our efforts to get away from adversity, we end up magnifying it, and it grows like a tick firmly attached to its host. When this happens, we end up swimming in an ocean of sorrow, sometimes for just a few moments and other times for years. As a society, we have a very limited view of how life should be, which is skewed in only one direction, towards what pleases us. This view is not in line with reality. In truth, there is no good without the bad. We wouldn't know bad if only good appeared, but by the same token, we wouldn't know good if only bad appeared. In fact, there is no inherent good or bad. These are both simply concepts with no real basis in reality.

We don't know what is going to happen from one moment to the next, thus we really can't say what is good or bad. There is a tale of a wise farmer whose horse ran off. When his neighbor came to console him about the lost horse the wise farmer said, "Who knows what's good or bad?" When the wise farmer's horse returned with a herd of horses following behind him, the foolish neighbor came over to congratulate the farmer on his good fortune. The wise farmer said, "Who knows what's good or bad?" Then when the wise farmer's son broke his leg trying to ride one of the new horses the foolish neighbor came to console him again. "Who knows what's good or bad?" said the wise farmer. When the army passed through signing men up for war, they passed over the farmer's son because of his broken leg. When the foolish neighbor came to congratulate the wise farmer on his son being spared, again the wise farmer said, "Who knows what's good or bad?"[23]

When we get something we want, we celebrate. When we get something we don't want, we get angry or may even cry. But often we will find that what we wanted turned out to be a disappointment, a burden, or even a terrible thing. Then when we get the thing we don't want, be it loss, illness, or an accident, we find it was the one thing that completely changed our lives for the better. In the midst of our experiences, we can't see the forest for the trees. So we can't emphatically say which experience is good or bad for us. Who knows? All we can do is be with what is happening in the moment.

Rabia al Basri was a poet and saint from the eighth century. It is said that when she was young, she was forced into the sex trade, becoming a sex slave until she was released around the age of fifty. Yet, she became known as one of the great female saints in the Islamic tradition. She was able to eloquently express her experience with God in her poetry. One of her poems indicates that she had an awakening experience that never left her. In another, she pointed out that most people get caught in the past by what they have seen, heard, or felt; they can't focus on the present. After she was released, people came to her for advice, and it was said she helped many.[24] Somehow, within what we all would consider her negative experience, she became free and was able to dance in the light of each moment, regardless of the challenges she faced.

Occasionally, adverse situations arise that overwhelm us. A spouse may leave for someone else, a sweet child dies, we lose our job, or maybe we even become homeless. Some people may be the victims of abuse, rape, torture, or other grievous situations. Once, I read about a family whose young daughter became ill with flu-like symptoms. When she became sicker and sicker, her parents took her to the hospital and discovered that she had a condition wherein the walls of the heart thin and eventually leads to death. The only long-term remedy was a heart transplant.

Fortunately, a heart became available for this little girl as a result of someone else dying. She was able to recover and live a normal life. However, a few years later, her little sister became sick and was diagnosed with the same condition. At the same time, her little brother also became sick and needed surgery on his heart. The parents had five children, and through these experiences and testing, they discovered that each of their five children had this condition, and all of them needed heart transplants.[25]

Of course, most of us aren't confronted with adversity as profound as I have just described. But when difficult circumstances arise, does it help us to drop into anger, despair, and anxiousness? Or would it be more helpful to be with what is happening and not add any additional mental noise to the experience? We all encounter plenty of other difficult circumstances. Sometimes these problems come to us one at a time, and occasionally they arrive in droves, staying well beyond our predetermined time limits. Of course, if we can do something about what arrives on the doorstep of our lives, we do it. But if there is nothing we can do to change it, then we each must deal with what is present. We could employ the same attitude as Rabia and be present with what is happening and not worry whether our current situation is bad or good.

Instead, of being challenged by overwhelming circumstances, we may live with a subtle yet irritating unease that lies under the surface of all of our experiences. We may find some temporary relief every now and again. Our vacation from work feels like freedom, our new lover brings us joy, but we wait in fear of what is approaching us from the land of the unknown, and all too soon, we are filled with feelings of dread or unhappiness. All of our lives, we have been trying new ways to outsmart these feelings. But what we have been doing throughout our lives may not be working.

We are frequently dissatisfied because most of the time we aren't getting what we want. We want good health and we get sick; we want love and we become an object of others' desires; we want to be old, but we are young; we want to be young, but the ravages of old age have caught up to us; we want happiness and we find sorrow. And even when we do get what we want, all too soon, we want more. We buy a new car and then immediately we need seat covers, rims, and a bike rack. We are rarely satisfied with our lives just as they are. What we don't want will arise without effort, making us even more unhappy. This unsatisfactory dance between grasping at positive experiences and averting negative ones makes up the content of our lives. Every moment, we are either getting what we want or we're not. And even if we are getting exactly what we want right now, at some level we know that it is bound to end. Whoever we may be, regardless of how good our lives are, rest assured sooner or later will all face adversity. How we deal with adversity can make the difference between a happy life and a sorrowful one.

Many of our habits for dealing with adversity are ineffectual. Maybe you've also stood in front of the refrigerator eating out of the ice cream container trying to drown your sorrows. It seems to work for as long as the ice cream sits on the tongue. Yet as soon as it melts, the spoon is already poised for another scoop. If you're like most people, the result of an ice cream binge is feelings of guilt and depression heaped on top of the original feeling of sadness or frustration. Eating through adversity doesn't work.

Another popular tactic for avoiding adversity is to run from it. We may do this physically by moving to a new country, traveling from place to place, leaving one lover for another, changing jobs, houses, spouses, or furniture. The problem with this is we take ourselves wherever we go. Since the problem isn't outside of us, there is no real escape by running. Sometimes we turn to drugs or alcohol to drown out life's dissatisfaction, but our problems simply multiply. Now instead of simply feeling jealousy, for example, we end up jealous, fat, and drunk. The cycle of suffering, samsara, continues to spiral, multiplying as we dive deeper into habitual patterns.

We get stuck in patterns of behavior that no longer work for us. Instead of falling into our habitual pattern of dealing with the abundant negative emotions we hold in our mental shopping cart, we can bring our attention inward and inquire into the basis of our suffering. Since emotions and thoughts are not external and are based in our minds, we can look into these perceptions and free ourselves.

The Buddha saw the plight we are all faced with when he left his palace and faced the world outside the palace gates. When he saw the overwhelming suffering of all beings, he sought a way beyond it. In his search to go beyond suffering, he spent years exploring the world inside himself. Initially, he practiced asceticism and eventually, he decided to go off alone, giving up the ascetic practices and sitting, simply looking into his mind. He sat under what is now called the Bodhi Tree, and when morning came, he realized the nature of reality. He saw the nature of suffering and the way out of suffering and then taught it for the remainder of his life.

The path to free ourselves requires seeing into what is happening in the moment, regardless of the bitterness or sweetness of the experience. Sitting with adversity is the path through it. There is nowhere to run and no place to hide. When we sit and drink tea with adversity, it is as if we are sitting with our most beloved teacher. We can pay attention to it and get to know it more intimately.

When adversity arises, we sit with it as a temporary guest in the house of our consciousness. This might sound scary to us—it may even sound crazy—but when we are able to look closely, without judging the experience as either good or bad, we will be able to transcend it. For example, if you think about a time when you were home late at night by yourself and you heard a strange sound, at first you might have been frightened, thinking someone was in the house. For an instant, you may have even been petrified. But as you paid closer attention or even went to investigate, what you probably found was the sound was only the wind, and upon realizing this, the fear immediately left. In the same way, when adversity arises, we may initially feel a sense of terror, but as we sit with the energy of the fearful response and get to know it, we will find that there was nothing to fear in the first place.

All forms of suffering are like a child's death in a dream," said Ngulchu Thogme.[26] Everything is empty; it is only through our deluded perception that we believe our experiences to be real. When this is realized, terror yields to deep calm. When we look into our habits in relationship to adversity, we can see what we have been doing doesn't work. Sometimes, if we are courageous and try something new, we are surprised by the positive outcome, and we wonder why we didn't try it a long time ago.

Let me tell a story one of my students recently shared with me about her experience with acceptance, or having tea with her teachers. She said every time she visited with her mom and dad, she ended up stressed and overwhelmed, flooded with feelings of inadequacy. For the longest time, she blamed these feelings on her parents. She felt that her parents were too judgmental, harsh, and strict. Since these feelings were so uncomfortable and continued over many years, she eventually decided to put her practice to work in her relationship with her parents. She resolved to watch what happened in her mind when she was with her parents. It wasn't easy and it took sustained effort, but eventually she was able to be with them just as they were. She still sometimes hears the harsh comments and notices the disapproving looks, but she no longer reacts in her previous manner. She sees the empty nature of her thoughts and is able to have tea with judgment and continue to experience harmony and peace. She feels happy to be able to have a new relationship with her experience.

We too can work with what we already have in our lives. If we really think about it, if we are experiencing adversity, it is already sitting on the couch of our consciousness. So there is no point in trying to lock the deadbolt to our hearts when difficult circumstances arise; instead, we can open our hearts and invite our teachers to tea.

7

An Unencumbered Life

We are encumbered not by things, people, ideas, or beliefs. We are encumbered by our attachment to them. We are especially attached to ego—our sense of self. To further complicate the matter, we make the roles we play define who we are, forgetting that they are only temporary roles. Most of us live our lives based on these roles. We can recognize that when we identify ourselves as this or that, it completely encumbers us. If we look closely, we will find we believe the story about ourselves we've been weaving throughout our lives. We've become attached to this story about who we are.

Instead, we could look at our lives differently and see the many roles we play, including parent, child, employee, victim, student, winner, loser etc. Just as an actor on a stage or in a movie takes on certain characters, we too are playing many roles for a little while. Sometimes we take on the role of super mom, best friend, husband, boss, or student. Sometimes we identify ourselves with something negative that has happened to us and become a victim. Even though there are many other aspects to us, we narrow ourselves down to this very small idea of who we are. Then we relate to the world through the eyes of a victim, and over and over we are victimized. We become encumbered by our ideas about our identity. Whatever role we identify with can become very real to us.

For example, I know someone who is a lovely person, but she has very limiting ideas about herself. She often talks about how no one pays attention to her. She says she isn't heard, and no one cares about her needs. One day I happened to be near her when she was trying to order food in a very crowded area. Rather than an organized line, there was a mob standing in front of the counter where she was trying to order. I could see that she was trying to get the attention of someone to place her order, but indeed, no one was paying attention to her. After watching this for a bit, I worked my way up to her. She complained to me again that no one would pay attention to her, and then I heard her try to call out to someone to take her order in the smallest, quietest voice. The sound she made barely went beyond her collar. She called out like this a few times, but no one responded. After watching this for a bit, I realized she was so identified with the idea she was not worthy of being heard that she could not speak up when needed. She could not put herself out there enough to be heard, but she didn't see this. Instead, she projected everything onto others and blamed the world for her misery.

Another person I know has spent the last eight years holding onto anger and grief because her husband left her. She was so attached to her identity as a wife that when he left, she felt he took her meaning, her heart, and her life from her. To this day, she is an angry person who is difficult to be around. Her attachment to her idea of who she is and her story about how her husband ruined her life has kept her from moving forward.

Maybe you can recognize the tendency to hold onto useless identifications. You may also see yourself as a victim, a self-identification that causes a lot of trouble. Maybe you have recognized this already or quite possibly you haven't yet looked into what you identify with and how it affects you. Let me ask, if a person identifies him/herself as a victim, how then can this person ever not be a victim? This perspective makes it impossible to go beyond this role. It is not until you become aware of what you are doing and then have the motivation to let go of your story that you will find relief.

What would it be like to no longer be a victim? What if one day we woke up and just walked away from that identification? Of course we can't walk away from what has happened to us and the impact it has had on us, but we can walk away from our identification with the label of who we are.

When we take on a label, we are really identifying with our ego. The problem with this is the misery it causes. If we can recognize this, we will have a lot of motivation to stop identifying so strongly with our idea of who we are. The value of labels is in our ability to communicate with one another, a sort of shorthand, without having to explain all the detailed nuances. We have to understand that the label and the roles we play are not a part of our inherent nature.

We can live full, unencumbered lives by freeing ourselves from these ideas and our stories. The only way any of our stories become real is if we make them real and then take on the attributes of that identification. How do we go beyond this? First we recognize it and then contemplate how it is manifesting in our lives. We start to do the experiment, the experiment of looking inward.

We can start to question the very strongly held ideas about who we are. *Is it beneficial to identify in this way? Is it serving me or humanity?* We can explore our relationship to the roles we play, thinking about what it would be like to let go of our identification with the self.

To go beyond limiting labels, we can look at how we've gotten hooked by the idea of who we are and how it has affected us. We can contemplate what we hear, read, or experience and ask ourselves these questions: *Is this true? Does it never vary? Is it true in all situations?* Because everything is dependent on something else and always changes, we can't answer yes to any of these questions. Everything is dependent on something else. Our perspectives are often very narrow and do not work in our favor. It is not helping us. It is not helping the world. When we look at the people who are causing harm in this world, we can see that they narrowly identify themselves and others. They may be identified with their height, weight, religion, race, gender, or the language they speak. Once we look closely, we see how ridiculous this is because it is so limiting.

We can get very caught up with ourselves as rich, smart, and better than others. This also causes harm. Ego can also be part of something that seems humble, but it really isn't, it is just ego. For example, when I was first ordained, I felt completely incapable of leading my first retreat. I found myself in tears the night before the retreat. I felt fearful, unworthy, and not good enough. This of course is also ego's game. Not too long into this game of the ego, Anam Thubten called from Hawaii. I told him, "I can't do this." He said something to the effect, "Oh, Dana, don't worry. You don't have to teach the Dharma. Just talk about the Dharma; just share it." I laughed and said, "Oh, okay. I can do that." When we identify with ourselves as some "thing," then we think we need to be a certain way and it limits us. Without the identification of Dharma teacher, I could see that I was only playing a role so the Dharma could be transmitted. If I didn't take on the role I had been given, then it would have been a disservice.

The ego can get caught in "I'm not good enough," or "I'm so good." Can we flow with what is happening in this moment? That is all we really need to do in this life. If we happen to be standing in front of a group of people who are called students, then maybe we play the role of teacher. It doesn't mean that everywhere we go we become the teacher. There is freedom in this lack of identification. There is openness. We can be everything or we can be nobody. We may not have a lot of money, but we don't have to identify ourselves as poor. If we have a lot of money, we don't have to identify ourselves as rich. You may have a lot of challenges in your life, but you don't have to identify yourself as someone who is challenged.

All we need to do is face what is in front of us right now and be with the experience of it without judgment. When we are open, when we are not identifying with ego, the natural, spontaneous wisdom that we are can arise. Often, we are churning through life making it a big struggle and life becomes so hard, but this is unnecessary. We aren't the label.

People sometimes get very nervous around talk of no self. They feel that they will disappear if they let go of the self. This is ego again. Ultimately, we can let go of our attachment to the self because it is just an idea. It is all just an idea about who we are. This is great news. With this perspective, we can start to relate to how life is presenting itself right now. How fun is that? It changes the whole ballgame. If the mind is creating the experience, how should it look? Free, open, moveable, flexible, and changeable, as life is? Or should it be rigid, concrete, and solid? It is up to us. As we work with our minds, we can explore the depth of who we are and the depth of life itself.

Through awareness, we not only see a more effective way to work with our lives and the challenges that are presented, but we also gain insight into the basis of all of our experiences and see the truth of the way things are. Our entire lives are transformed by abiding in awareness. We gain a new perspective, a new way of seeing, that is liberating. Like a lotus that grows in mud and lays so beautifully on the surface of the water, we too can thrive in the challenges that life brings, and the truth can shine through us.

To go deeply into all of life's experiences, it helps to be willing to see the entirety of what resides within our minds. Sometimes the search may be challenging. It may be like examining a deep wound, which is not so easy to look into for most of us. A psychological wound often contains fear and self-loathing. We might not want to inspect what we consider the negative aspects of ourselves. Instead, we may want to shield ourselves from what we think we will see. We may want to avoid scrutinizing the dark crevasses of our inner worlds. Initially, we tiptoe towards our wounded hearts and tentatively glance inward. Or, if we are brave or very motivated, we may be able to take a long, deep look inside to see what is there. Either way, it is helpful to look at the emotions that arise when we look inward. We can ask: *What am I running from? What is there to be afraid of? What is below the surface of this experience?* When we are brave enough to venture into the dark cave of our inner worlds, we will be able to see the psychological baggage that we carry. Through seeing, we are already liberating ourselves from our baggage, our wounded hearts, and our illusions.

We learn that underneath everything we experience in the mind is luminosity. So it is not the depressing experience that we might have thought it was going to be. When we look deeply, we see past our concepts and labels. We can see our experiences nakedly, which liberates us from all the constraints our small minds have imagined into being.

8

No I in You

When I first met my teacher, Anam Thubten Rinpoche, I used to carry a spiral-bound notebook to every retreat, so I could take notes in anticipation of reading them over again and again to be reminded of the teachings. I ended up not really going back to the notes once I was back home again, yet with each new retreat I would purchase a new spiral notebook and take notes again. I have a particular system for note taking. Whenever I feel something is very important, I write it out in large letters and put a few stars around it for emphasis. A while back, I decided to look over the large stack of notebooks that had accumulated over the years. I did this for a couple of reasons, one was out of nostalgia and the other was to see what I used to think was important when hearing a Dharma talk. I had to laugh out loud when I leafed through notebook after notebook because what I found in every notebook in large letters, sometimes taking up a quarter of the page, was: ***There is no I in you!***

In the beginning, I had no idea of what this meant, but I continued to write it and contemplate it.

Our strong sense of separateness from others and the world around us creates a belief in duality that is so tenacious, we fall victim to thinking what we experience is indeed solid and real. We then react to life with aversion and craving, always trying to get what we want and avoid what we don't want. The basis for this ignorance is that we think *somebody* is home—a solid and sustaining entity, a self, an ego, or we can call it the "I." However, there is no I in you. In other words, there isn't a "somebody" or an ego within us that is directing us. In some sense, there is nobody home.

We have static ideas, but we haven't really investigated those ideas. Neuroscientists are attempting to understand the brain–body relationship and are discovering new things all the time. According to science writers, Sandra and Matthew Blakeslee, the brain has an entire map of the body. In fact, the most recent research indicates that there are many maps related to sensations, emotions, etc. The body map extends past what we consider to be our body into the space around our body, which they call peripersonal space. This space is elastic and contracts and expands in order to be most effective in negotiating our world. Even our body does not exist how we think it does. Our sense is that it ends where our flesh ends, but the research indicates that's not the case. Instead of ending where our flesh ends, peripersonal space blends with the world, including other beings. In addition, this space is contracting and expanding in every moment; we just don't realize it.[27] Paul Brooks, a Neuropsychologist, says that self is an illusion akin to a story that we weave over time.[28] Science is only beginning to explore this area, and already it is showing us that how we think things are, is different than they actually are.

Thousands of years prior to these scientific discoveries, the Buddha saw the illusory nature of the self. Of course, though neuroscientists and the Buddha said this, it doesn't make the self any less real to us. Unless we have training and insight into our true nature, we will not *know* this truth for ourselves; it will remain only a concept. Through inquiry, we can look into the idea of the self directly. Without investigation, we will continue to live deluded by the idea that there is separation between "I" and experience, between you and me, between us and the wholeness of everything as if there is a mini self, a mini me who directs, judges, desires, and pushes away those things it doesn't like and grabs onto what it likes. Indeed, most people spend their whole lives tightly clinging to this sense of a self, this "I-ness." However, no matter how strongly we cling to this notion of an "I," it doesn't exist. This notion of an inherently existing "I," a mini me inside, is a false construct based on our thoughts and imaginations. In truth, there is no realness to the "I."

The wisdom teachings on emptiness encourage us to look directly into the nature of the mind, so we can see into its empty nature. When we drop everything, what is remaining to suffer about? In that moment, we have already transcended our neurosis. Since the "I" is only a thought, when we drop it, we see there is no one there to resist.

The thought of letting go of the self can feel scary, yet we have done it many times when we were completely absorbed in a sunset or looking into the eyes of a loved one. Those moments are so beautiful because we are fully experiencing the richness of life, and we aren't judging it, manipulating it, intellectualizing it, or comparing it. Instead, we are fully present. Another way to relate to this is by thinking of expanding our hearts and minds so wide, infinitely, to include all of life's experiences. Then, it really doesn't matter if we think of the self or not, we can contain all of our experiences and the world without mental resistance.

We are composed of five aggregates: form, feeling, perception, formation, and consciousness. Form refers to the material world, including our body. There are three kinds of feelings: pleasant, unpleasant, and neutral. Perception is how we interpret the world around us. Formations are mental formations, which include thoughts, concepts, and beliefs. Lastly, for simplicity sake, the consciousness can be defined as the ability to be aware of what is happening in the moment.

It seems as though the combination of aggregates contains a solid and real self. However, as we investigate each of these aggregates individually, they do not have any substantiality to them. In other words, the aggregates that make up this form are empty of a self. Although we may speak of a self as convention, a way to communicate with one another, there is no self within or apart from the aggregates.

To experiment with this personally, we can look into each of these aggregates through meditation to see if the self is located within them. We can start by looking at our bodies because this is where the sense of self is so firmly attached. Shantideva pointed out that if we cut through the fibers of a banana tree, we find nothing;[29] likewise, through investigation, we will find no "I," no underlying self. He went on to point out that our bodies, though seeming to be substantial, are actually made up of parts, and those parts, such as feet, hands, fingers, and so on, are made up of atoms, and atoms have no inherent existence. We are attached to something that is like a rainbow or a dream—it appears momentarily but has no inherent existence. When looking for the "I," we will not find anything.

Even when we look into feelings, perceptions, mental formations, and the consciousness, we can't find the "I." If we can't find the "I" within the aggregates, than we can't expect it to be in the combination of the aggregates, the being. This would be like mixing copper and iron together and expecting gold to be present. If gold is not present in the beginning within either copper or iron, then we can't expect it to be present when the elements are combined.

In addition, there seems to be a continuation of the entity we call "I." We say, "I learned something new," or "I went to the store," or "I am good." The point we miss is that "I" doesn't truly exist; it is a convention of language, as well as an idea, about being separate. But, it is not who we are. We can transcend the notion of a continuous "I" by realizing that it is an illusion. Moment by moment we let go of the self, the ego. The ego soon builds itself back up, like the cartoon character Wile E. Coyote, who pops back up after being squashed by an Acme safe to chase the Roadrunner again; and when that happens, we let it go again.

The Buddha mentioned that this body is not ours, nor does it belong to others. It should be seen as a product of history. We are much bigger than this limited form. When we see that our essence is awareness itself, then we see there aren't any limitations for us.

The simplest approach is to rest in the natural state of mind. This is an unelaborated approach, meaning we are not "doing" anything when we rest in the natural state of mind. Instead of doing, we engage in nondoing. This is not the nondoing of putting our feet on the coffee table and drinking a beer; rather, it is the act of letting the structure of our ego unravel itself by simply being present. An analogy for this is found in muddy water. If we take a glass of muddy water and stir it up, the water and mud create a cloudy effect.

However, if we leave the muddy water alone, the mud will settle to the bottom and the water will clear. Like this, if we leave the mind alone sitting in awareness, the mind naturally clears, and we can see its luminous nature. The mind has never been tainted by anything that has crossed through it. Like a movie screen, the screen is unaffected by the display upon it.

We can come home to the moment with awareness, and in so doing, the truth unveils its luminous nature to us. All we need to do is let go of our striving, grasping, and aversion so we can rest. Meditation is not about creating a better self; it is about letting things be as they are in their ultimate nature—*free.*

If we consistently sit like this, we will eventually find the "I" drops away on its own. The self is no longer a part of the equation. When we stop *doing,* we find that what we have been trying to protect, defend, and inflate was never real in the first place.

The whole thing is like an illusion. As a magician deceives his audience into thinking his magic tricks are real, we have been deceived into the idea that we must continually establish and then guard the self. This delusion has been the source of so much sorrow. When I was younger I spent a lot of money on self-help books and programs in order to work on myself, and it really didn't help me much. How funny it is to think about this now. It is as if I had an invisible friend who was full of neurosis, which I worried about, spent money on and tried fixing, when it never existed in the first place.

There is no "I" inside us. It is not found anywhere. Our perspective is born out of habits we have been conditioned into, but there is no real existence to it. We are told "to transcend the self and let it go." In truth, however, there really isn't a self to transcend, since it never existed in the first place. What we end up transcending is a thought about a self. In this way, realization is exposed rather than created. In other words, we don't have to deconstruct a self that has never been in existence in the first place. Seeing this truth is transcendent wisdom. The heart of the Dharma is the experience of this truth.

9

Dive into the Ocean of Love

I don't think there is a person on this earth who doesn't want to feel loved. We search for people to love us online, in synagogues, temples, churches, workplaces, and bars to name a few. We want love from our friends and family, yet it is as if we are drinking saltwater and are left thirsty, not finding satisfaction. Our search for the perfect mate leads many of us on an all-out hunt for the person who can make us feel loved. Although our search is sometimes punctuated with moments of great bliss, the bliss doesn't last. Our search leads us in the wrong direction; we mistakenly look outside of ourselves for what we already possess.

There is an ocean of love we can dive into at any time. It is our very essence. This love has no reference point, and it is not directed towards anyone or any particular thing; it is simply being love itself. Recognizing the depth of being, we become great lovers of the truth. It is the sublime act of opening our hearts to everything.

We don't need to manufacture love through effort. Maybe you can remember the first moment you fell head-over-heels in love with your child. Can you remember back to that moment when your child was placed in your arms for the first time? When this happened, you didn't have to cultivate a feeling of love; instead, it arose spontaneously and pervaded your entire being. This love didn't have to be cultivated or dredged up from some place. In other words, it wasn't work. You didn't have to try to feel love or create a loving experience. It arose on its own while you were fully present in the moment. The preoccupation with the self dropped away and all that remained was love.

I remember experiencing this with my own children. The moment they were placed in my arms, a deep love spontaneously arose and left an indelible imprint on my heart. In that moment, I would have done anything, even fight an army of warriors to protect my child from harm. You may not have children and can instead remember when you first fell in love with your boyfriend or girlfriend. Everything was bliss; the world was covered with rainbows, and joy ruled your heart. It seemed that all your dreams had come true, the butterflies in your stomach and the warmth in your heart arose with just the thought of your beloved.

A while ago, someone told me he had found the perfect person. He listed off her attributes and how those matched up with his desires, but already the relationship is over and feelings of disappointment and anger have taken their place. Romantic love is entangled with expectation and attachment. It is not pure love. Even the love we have for our children can become filled with attachment if we aren't mindful.

There is an even deeper reservoir of love that sits in our hearts, a pristine love that is untainted by our grasping and clinging. We have access to this reservoir because it always resides within, and it is not dependent on someone. We can experience this great love, not through striving, but through letting go of our attachment to ourselves. Then, the ego ceases, dropping away, and without effort we dive into the ocean of love.

Fortunately, we don't have to meet Mr. or Mrs. Right to access this love. And it is not something that we achieve after a good deal of hard work. Love is here, right now, in this moment, completely accessible to anyone. Yet, most people don't know this reservoir of love exists. And if they do have some sense of it, they often feel that it has to be earned through hard work or by becoming good enough. This notion of earning love by being good enough causes us so much misery. Although it seems very spiritual and maybe even wise, it isn't. There are many who have fallen into this pit. Although the pit seems to be lined with gold, it is still a pit.

The idea of being "good enough" is a dualistic notion. Embedded in this idea is a sense that something is wrong with us that needs to be fixed before we can experience love or give love to others. Our experience of not feeling loveable may seem as though there is a hole in the center of our bodies that is incapable of being filled: a bottomless abyss, a dark and scary place that lingers like a black hole, sucking the joy out of life.

This all sounds very dramatic, but this was my personal experience prior to meeting with the teachings of this path. I thought I wasn't good enough, and I felt miserable much of the time. One day when I felt terrible and this hole in my gut seemed to be extremely powerful, I decided to stick with the feeling, even though it was scary. This time I didn't mentally run from the experience. Instead, I paid attention to the feelings that arose in relation to this hole. Suddenly, the insight arose in me that there wasn't a hole. In fact, I realized simultaneously there never was a hole and I had always been good enough. I wasn't lacking a thing. At that point, I started laughing out loud at the absurdity of my belief in a hole in the first place. This sudden insight was so powerful that I have never felt the presence of that hole again. The release from this feeling was due to being in awareness and the insight that the hole was empty of any inherent existence; it was unreal. In fact, the hole was a thought. I was released from its hold when I let go.

Many people seek a spiritual path because they think they are not good enough, and they believe the path is about working to become better so they can become worthy. The truth is that each of us is already good enough because we are already love. We are the wholeness of everything, the depth of the well of love—there is no way to earn it, just as we don't need to earn being a human being because this is what we are.

When we experience love, free from attachment, it is our true nature we are experiencing. Sometimes, we mistakenly project this onto others, but love is our true face and has always been ours since the beginning of time. We may not yet have realized this truth, but we can have confidence that this is the truth and live as if we already fully know this about ourselves.

For those who view themselves as limited, it may feel as though a lot of effort is needed to love themselves and others. People often ask me how they can give love to others and not deplete themselves, as if there is a limited amount of love inside them. But love is not doled out in finite amounts.

It is not like having one candy bar that needs to be shared with others in bite-sized pieces in order for it to last. Love is infinite; the reservoir is bottomless. Since we are inherently love, there is no need to worry about how much we have already given. In fact, through giving, our capacity to love expands.

How do we fall in love? The easiest way is to rest in the natural state of the mind. When we fall in love, the dance of the divine springs forth, and we find no preference for one thing over another or desire to make the universe different. We can see, as the great saints saw that love is with us always, even when we don't feel we have access to it. When we recognize this truth, we are not caught in the duality of self and other or good and bad. Those who have this realization fall in love with themselves, humanity, and life itself. In this sense, love is not directed at anyone in particular; instead, it includes everything. Dualistic ideas drop away and we can relate to the world without preference. Ultimately, we can see the nature of awareness as emptiness.

To experience this truth of emptiness, we may choose to take a vacation from our everyday habits. We don't have to travel far. We can go inside because true understanding is uncovered through insight. Eventually, we will experience love permeating our awareness.

When we sit in meditation, we find that our minds begin to feel calmer and our hearts open wider. We become free from the tight constraints of our thinking minds. When we are able to sit with the experience and not put up a fuss rejecting what we are thinking or what is happening in our lives, we can find a sense of relief and even taste freedom. It doesn't take elaborate practices in order to realize this love. Like an ice cube that melts on a warm surface, we can melt our frozen ideas about ourselves and the world around us.

We don't need to strive to experience this love. We can just let go of trying to secure ourselves and melt.

This doesn't mean we don't need to put forth some effort. When the clouds sit low in the valley obscuring the blue sky and the bright sun, we drive to higher ground to break through the inversion, which takes effort. Like this, ultimate love reveals itself when we put enough effort forth to look. If we are ready and have cleared away what has been covering our view, we may see this for ourselves.

Letting go of our limiting beliefs, expectations, and stories about life and simply being present with the flow of life itself is letting go. Can you imagine what it would feel like to be free of all limiting beliefs? It might feel like dancing naked in the streets. We don't need to drop our clothes; rather, we can drop our beliefs and experience our true nature. When we no longer cling to a false self, the idea of a separate self, we are able to see everything as the expression of awareness. With this realization, we are freed from inner and outer enemies. You may remember the story of the Buddha's awakening. He saw the truth of his experience: there is no inherent self or other, and all appearances are like a dream. Through this realization, he was able to experience the nature of the mind and go beyond his conditioned mind.

When we can be with what is happening right now, instead of believing our projections about future calamities, we can pause and fall in love with what's happening in our lives right now. It is letting go that allows us to recognize the infinite reservoir of love. In this way, all the negative power is taken away from the situation. When we cut through our grasp on people, beliefs, and so on, we allow the fullness of life to flow into our hearts. Every time someone pushes our buttons, it's an opportunity to try out these principles.

We can choose how we're going to respond. Some days, we may respond out of habit, but every once in a while, we may respond in awareness and surprise ourselves with how wonderful it is to be free from our habitual patterns. We can encourage ourselves to try to see life differently, to look for the extraordinary in all of life. We can take the nondualistic view that everything is already perfect as it is. As this realization pervades our everyday lives, we begin to experience a sense of freedom from the heavy weight of habits; we may even realize there isn't a problem. There's only this open pristine moment.

Once we decide we have had enough of suffering, we enter the path and work to alleviate our suffering and the suffering of others. Sometimes we have powerful moments of insight and are able to see life in a new way; however, we often have the experience of gaining insight and then falling into delusion. We repeat this process again and again. It sometimes feels like going forward two steps and then falling back three, but eventually, we are able to see even this as a story.

Practice is the key. Without it, we are easily overwhelmed by the smallest of challenges. The best time to practice is now. We can sit on our meditation cushion, letting the ego drop away and fall in love. When we meditate, we can watch what comes up again and again, and each time we recognize that we are lost in our thoughts; we reside for that moment in awareness.

Life is inviting us to live fully and to wake up to its wholeness. We can compare it to a parent who tries to wake up a teenager in the morning. In the beginning, the parent taps lightly saying, "Come on, it's time to get up for school." But by the fifth time the parent barges in the room and shakes the teenager's arm yelling, "Wake up!" Like this, we may be challenged frequently until we give up all of our usual strategies for trying to fix or get around life.

When we open to life, we can see that we are not conditioned to the truth. In truth, nothing is separate from love. We can learn to see the extraordinariness in all those we meet. Love spontaneously arises when we drop our fixation on ourselves, and love becomes its own reward. We begin to shift out of our current, unsuccessful paradigm and move towards a fuller view. Then, when someone is rude and unhelpful, we will be able to see this person as a gift who is teaching patience. These opportunities are everywhere, yet we often miss them. We can also take the advice Rumi gave in his poem, "Relationship Booster," and we can meet everyone with our eyes lit up as if we have heard the most brilliant words falling from their lips.[30] "What's for dinner?" could become the fuel for our awakening, and our response can fill the heart of the wise one who spoke those words. When we fall in love with the wholeness of life, our hearts dance regardless of the presentations from the outer world because we know the truth that we are never separate from love—it is the nature of everything.

Whatever you find as an obstacle or challenge in your life, embrace it. Become a resting place for those in need. Fall in love with all of life, and keep falling in love with it, recognizing it as the dance of awareness itself. Open your heart and open your mind and dive into the ocean of love.

10

It's Enough!

When I was a child, my family always drove to our vacation destination. My mom and dad would load us all up into the station wagon in the early morning hours before the sun rose and start down the road. My mom always packed bags and bags of groceries to keep our mouths stuffed, our bellies full, and our hands occupied. She also knew that if she didn't pack food for all of us, we might actually have starved to death because my dad was not fond of stopping the car for us to eat, use the bathroom, or stretch our legs. This was during a time when fast food wasn't an option. If you are young, this may be impossible to imagine, but I assure you there was a time when people had to go into a restaurant and sit down to get a meal. Nevertheless, it was only when the station wagon needed more fuel to continue down the road that my dad would stop the car. He had a single goal—get there! After numerous hours (well, it seemed like numerous hours to me, but it could have been just two), one of us kids would ask, "Are we there yet?"

My dad would reply, "Not yet." And then when asked the natural follow-up question, "How much longer?" he would say, "forty-five minutes." It could have been hours, minutes, or seconds before we arrived but we always received the same answer: forty-five minutes. "Get there" was the attitude permeating the entirety of our station wagon.

This attitude may work for a car trip, but it doesn't work very well for our lives. Yet many of us employ this same attitude. We put off enjoying our lives for some future goal at some future date. This attitude creeps into our work life, family life, and our spiritual life. In our work life, we strive for the day we can retire and then really have fun. After our children are born, we look forward to seeing them meet milestones along the way: sitting at six months, pulling themselves up by nine months, walking by twelve months, reading by age five, and moving out by age eighteen. We put everything into striving and working until that glorious day when we have enough.

Do you ever feel like a hamster running on a spinning wheel trying to get somewhere and never arriving? It's exhausting, isn't it? At least the hamster is getting exercise. We, on the other hand, only become mentally fatigued. We may think it is necessary to run on the wheel of life, pushing ourselves to be better, to get more, and to have it all. However, our premise for running on this wheel is fundamentally incorrect. It will not bring us anything that lasts, and we aren't really getting anywhere.

If we are striving to get somewhere in our spiritual lives, we are applying the same approach to the rest of our life activities. In fact, striving becomes a serious hindrance. The reason for this is our spiritual lives are not separate from life, and life is happening only in this moment. So, this moment is really the only moment we can be in; any other moment is only a story about the past, or in the case of "are we there yet," the future.

When we are striving, it is as if we are trying to conquer something, like conquering a mountain by climbing to the top. If we take this attitude in our spiritual lives, we will never get to the top of the mountain. It will be like a mirage that moves further away from us. Just as there is no capturing a mirage, we can't capture liberation. It will always elude us if we attempt to grasp it.

This doesn't mean we give up our spiritual life, meditation, or other spiritual activities. We still take action and participate in the activities that allow us to grow and change. But instead of living for the end point, we simply are present for the journey.

Striving is full of struggle, which perpetuates our habitual tendencies. When we strive to get something, we struggle and fight against life. If we take a different attitude, one of being present rather than future oriented, we simply enjoy the path, noticing the view along the way. This is a much different attitude. In this way, we can be with whatever is happening at any point along the trail. However, with the attitude of getting somewhere, we can only be happy when we have achieved our goal—when we have conquered. Then what happens? Once we have conquered, are we perpetually happy or do we then strive towards some other goal, something else to conquer to be happy again? This is why we continually strive, because we aren't ever satisfied for long.

When we have an attitude of striving in our spiritual life, we may become tortured by thoughts: *I didn't have a good meditation today; I should already be liberated; hopefully, I'll have a good meditation tomorrow; I need to meet with the highest teacher; I once had a blissful experience, and I need to create it again.* We can make the path into a challenge, a competition, an ego game, rather than the purpose it is meant to assume. Our striving can easily become misdirected. We can end up torturing ourselves on our spiritual path with guilt and worry. Only by paying close attention to our motivations will we be able to come back to the moment again and again, rather than get caught up in the future or stuck in the past.

The path is simply about being aware in our everyday experiences, so we can see the truth of the moment. It is about being there for our ordinary lives. It's not about getting to the top of something; it is more about being with life as it is presented. With direct perception, we transcend our stories about life. There is really nothing to get. We can learn to be with life, rather than thinking about life, which separates us from life itself.

The point isn't to get rid of, trample, suffocate, repress, or shut down what is arising in the mind. We can think about cute kittens, a horror film, sunny days when it is raining, or snowy days when it is too hot. The point is to recognize the profound nature of the mind itself. When we recognize the nature of the mind, we see that it is luminous and untainted by what is appearing, and we are no longer under the influence of the various appearances. Instead, we can engage with them as the appearances they are. We can see the complex, dynamic, and rich aspects of all of life and be touched by its fullness and live it fully no matter the outer circumstances.

To live this kind of life requires training the mind. Otherwise, an untrained mind gets led around like a cow that is pulled by a ring in its nose. I once had a student in one of my classes in high school who thought of himself as very tough. He liked to box and was very proud of himself.

One day, a fly was buzzing around in my classroom. This student became very annoyed and kept trying to kill the fly with anything on hand. When he left his seat to kill the fly I reminded him that in my classroom, we don't kill insects. When I said this, he was flabbergasted. He couldn't believe that I wanted him to let the fly live and continue to land on him and torture him so much. He might have been able to take a punch, but his mind was tortured by a tiny fly. Of course, this young man was not unusual in wanting to rid himself of discomfort. We have all spent time shooing flies away from us, and we all want to be comfortable. When we are unaware, even the smallest of things can become a source of mental torture.

It is easy to lose awareness and to get involved in the goal of trying to get rid of negative situations. Instead of trying to get rid of something, we can try to sit with what is happening for just a little while. Can we sit with the fly, with fear, with wanting but not getting? Because when we can just sit, we will find freedom arising, not because we are getting something, but because we are able to stop fighting with life's current presentation.

Try it out for yourself by taking a moment to reflect back on an experience you've had today. Did you notice you wanted more? Did you want more time off, more family, more dessert, more meaning, or more friendship? Desire can sometimes be rather subtle, and we aren't always attuned to the more subtle aspects of ourselves.

Looking back over the week, you may have had only a few brief moments of feeling you have enough or are enough. It may seem that nothing is enough. Let's experiment by taking a moment to sit quietly and be with the sounds of our body, the sounds in the room, sensations, and thoughts. Don't try to change anything—just be. Don't strive to do something. "Being" is a present-moment experience. It is being present with whatever is happening right now. If it is cold out, we can be present with that experience. When it is hot out, we can be present with that experience. If we are resisting any of these circumstances, we can be with resistance. Of course, if something is changeable, then we can change it, but if we can't change it, then we are creating friction in our mind stream between what we want and what we have, which leaves a painful residue in our consciousness. In other words, we are creating confusion and pain for ourselves. On a cold day, we can put on layers of clothing, stay inside, or make a fire, but we can't change the cold temperature outside. If we have to be outside, then we can accept the weather just as it is and be present with the experience of the cold.

Life is arising in every moment, but there is a layer of constant chatter and judgment about our life experiences that keeps us from seeing the inherent beauty of life. It is as if we have a person standing outside of us, or split personalities, one side judging the other. It reminds me of how ice skating was judged years ago: one moment is a 9.2 experience, and the next moment is a 3.0 experience. The small mind is always judging. With every thought arising, we think, *This is a good experience. This is a 7.5 experience, but I really wanted a 9.5 experience.* We may think, *I'm good. I'm bad. This thought is good; that thought is bad.* We end up unhappy and confused.

Instead, if we just experience life, we are able to sit with it and experience its perfection as it is. When we let go of the conceptual mind that makes these nuanced judgments, we are freed. We may not be freed permanently, but we are freed momentarily from the pain of resisting what is. The experience of the present moment is always available to us.

We only need to be there for it. In other words, we only need to be aware. Awareness, the naturally occurring unfettered display, is always available. By dropping a dualistic view of self and other, good and bad, desirable and undesirable, the stream of awareness is experienced. Abstract solidity and the crystallization of the experience drop away, and all that remains is pure presence.

Striving actually keeps us from experiencing what is. There is a parable about a man who led a donkey through a border checkpoint every day for thirty years. The guards at the checkpoint were suspicious that the man was trying to smuggle something into the kingdom, but every time they searched the old man and the packs the donkey carried, they came up empty-handed. The man continued to cross the border day after day, always leading his donkey. The only thing that changed was that he wore more expensive clothes. After thirty years, one of the border guards retired. One day, he saw the old man in town and begged him to tell him what he had been smuggling for all those years. He swore to the old man that he would not tell anyone, he just needed to know for himself. The old man said, "Since you can no longer arrest me, I will tell you. I was smuggling donkeys."[31]

So you see, sometimes what we are looking for is right under our nose, but we are unable to see it when we are striving. The truth is in our present-moment experience. As pointed out in the Prajnaparamita Sutra, "The whole world is the insubstantial play of universal enlightenment. It is all simply suchness, inextinguishable and indistinguishable simplicity."[32]

Everything is already enlightened, so we can stop trying to make life be anything other than it is right now. By performing mental gymnastics, attempting to bend and twist our minds into the shape we think they should be bent into, we inadvertently perpetuate confusion. Those who are trying to awaken are very prone to this malady. Because we feel we need to be more than we are, we strive to change our experience and our thoughts. There is a strong tendency to believe we can think our way into being holy beings. When this happens, we may become stuck on the surface of our lives, unable to experience its richness.

We confuse ourselves in other ways. Once I overheard someone say that the Dharma was essentially positive thinking. I'm afraid that many people may have this misperception. Even though this may appear to be the case at first glance, it isn't positive thinking. Although I feel positive thinking is beneficial, awareness is much more profound; it goes to the heart of all of our experiences, be they positive or negative. With insight, we can see that no matter what thoughts cross the screen of our consciousness, it is empty, meaning thoughts are neither positive nor negative on their own.

Machik Labdrön, a heroine of mine, was an eleventh century awakened Tibetan Buddhist woman who wrote a "Doha,"[33] a song of realization, which speaks directly to what I am trying to elucidate here. She began the song, "Uprisings, apparitions, evidence of success are just mind's labels, they never existed." In other words, by attaching a label to thought, which is based on our conditioned perception, we end up believing the thought to be positive or negative. However, by simply seeing the empty nature of thought, we are not influenced by it. The same is true of our experiences, emotions, and sensations. In other words, we don't have to change a negative thought into a positive thought. We only need to see that each thought is empty.

Aryadeva, another great master, pointed out, "He who sees the nature of one thing will see the suchness of everything."[34] For the emptiness of one thing is the emptiness of everything. When we dive fully into the truth of the way things are, we see that all phenomena are ineffable; everything is subjective and is always changing.

On New Year's Day, I saw a post on Facebook from a young lady. She wrote that her boyfriend had fallen asleep at 8:30 p.m., and she was feeling all alone on New Year's Eve. She had been looking at pictures others had posted on Facebook, showing happy couples out on the town celebrating the new year, and initially, this made her feel lonely and left out. However, instead of dwelling on this feeling, she decided to have some fun with it. So she lay down next to her boyfriend, and with a smile on her face, snapped the picture of the two of them together. Now, I'm not sure if she was able to see the empty nature of her thoughts; however, she was able to change her perception about them and her sadness dissipated. She could also have been with her experience of sadness and noticed the texture, the pulse, the color of it, and she would have seen the empty nature of it.

It is easy to think that we need to improve everything, including ourselves. There are many forces in the world that perpetuate this kind of thinking. However, I would like to propose that we are enough, our experience is enough, and we no longer need to strive for a different experience, a different self, or different thoughts. Awareness allows us to see the games we play. We will then be able to look into our thoughts, experiences, and sensations, see their empty nature, and they will transform themselves through insight. It is a great relief to drop the processes of bringing the self to life. Once we imagine it into life, it takes a lot of effort to sustain it and protect it.

When we are striving, it is as though we are wearing all the clothing in our closet. As we gain insights into the nature of reality, we may be fortunate enough to strip off all the layers at once and abide in our true nature. However, the path for most of us is not as simple as stripping off our clothes. Instead, it may be a bit more like struggling up the ninety-nine switchbacks on Mt. Whitney, going back and forth over and over again until we finally reach the top. Like this, it may take us more time to begin to strip off the layers of delusion. In the beginning, it may be easy to recognize the bulky sweatshirts of anger, hatred, and jealousy. But as we strip off more and more layers, they become much more subtle, very fine layers of concepts.

As we climb towards the pinnacle of realization and the gross layers of neurosis have dropped away, we may think we are ready to throw our leg over the top of the mountain and take our place as a liberated being. If we have insight, we may see that we are not yet naked but continue to wear the gossamer concept of trying to be better, or the chiffon concept of needing to change ourselves, or maybe only the fine ribbon of attachment to liberation. If we realize, truly see, that all of what I have described just now is mind-made, then we will have glimpsed the truth. We will see that we have always been free; we just didn't yet have the perspective to see it for ourselves.

It is not possible to make ourselves good enough when our nature is already pristine. It is like trying to make pure white whiter. We could spend years trying to make pure white whiter. Indeed, we could spend lifetime after lifetime trying to do this, but if it is already pure white, then we are wasting precious time and energy. Similarly, we are already liberated—we just don't know it. It is not that we need to do something; it would be more accurate to say we only need to see this truth for ourselves. We perform mental gymnastics and become so tied up into knots that at some point we get so exhausted that we let everything go. Through letting everything go, we experience we are enough.

This present mind is Buddha-mind. Remember, the term "Buddha" means "one who is awake." The nature of the mind is an awakened mind. Look into your mind right now without any preconceived notions, and maybe you can see this for yourself. According to the great masters who have walked this path before us, we are effortlessly complete; there is no need for striving. We are enough!

This is the perfect moment. Nothing is happening. When we rest in this, we see this for ourselves: we find that we have arrived. In fact, we are there already and have always been there. We just didn't realize it.

11

Living with an Awakened Heart

Twenty-seven years ago, on the first day of kindergarten my son stood in line with all the other bright young faces waiting to board the school bus. However, before he could take his first step into the bus he fainted. As he roused himself his dad picked him up and carried him onto the bus. At that point he was crying and pressing his tear stained face against the bus window looking out at us standing on the street. I was not happy about this turn of events so, ran back home, got in my car and followed the bus on its way to the school. While I followed the bus, a boy sitting by my son who was also starting kindergarten that day reached out to comfort him. He moved beside my little boy, draped his arm across his shoulders and told him, "Don't worry, I know everything about this school. My sister went there. It will be alright, I'll show you everything."

By the time the bus arrived at school my son was laughing, talking to others looking perfectly content. He was so engaged with others he didn't see my face pressed against the glass of his classroom door assuring myself that he was alright. That young boy who reached out with care and compassion made a huge difference in my son's life. He is still one of my son's best friends, twenty-seven years later.

As you can see, little acts of compassion can affect a lifetime. Every compassionate act makes a difference in some way to the recipient. The more people we touch with our love and compassion, the better all of our lives will become. In Buddhist terminology, a genuine concern for all sentient beings is known as *bodhichitta*. The term *bodhi* means awakened and *chitta* is the Sanskrit word for mind/heart. Bodhichitta can be translated as "one with an awakened heart." A heart like this is capable of being present with suffering and feels a strong desire to relieve suffering wherever it is found. An awakened heart is a powerful heart that goes beyond traditional ideas of compassion. An awakened heart belongs to those who are considered *bodhisattvas*. Bodhisattvas direct their activity towards awakening for the benefit of all beings. These aren't mythical beings; they may even be our neighbors or strangers on the street. They are ordinary people who have dedicated themselves to working for the benefit of other beings without concern for themselves.

When listening to the radio one day, I heard about Coast Guard divers who were dispatched to rescue a whale. When they approached the whale, they could see she was barely floating on the surface of the ocean. When they were able to get closer, they found the whale was entangled in several thousand pounds of crab trap lines. The enormous weight of these lines was threatening to pull her down into the deep ocean. She looked to be nearly out of energy and was struggling to stay on the surface so she could breathe.

As with most humpbacks whales, this one was about the size of a large bus. They estimated that she was about fifty tons. With some trepidation but with great courage, the men jumped into the water, took out their knives, and started hacking away at the ropes. The whale was initially fearful of the divers and made some threatening motions with her fin, which was the size of an airplane wing, but the divers continued forward to try to disentangle her. The rope covered one of the whale's eyes, cut into her body in many places, and was extremely entangled around her tail. The divers felt the situation was pretty hopeless. They really didn't feel that the rescue would be a success, yet they continued to try to free the whale, risking their own lives to help this sentient being. One of the divers said that when he was cutting the rope away from the whale's eye, the whale kept watching him as he moved. It took about an hour to cut the whale free.

Finally, with the last cut, the cages and rope floated down into the abyss, and the divers came to the surface, cheering and hollering, thrilled to have been able to free the whale. Then one of the divers looked down and saw the whale coming up right underneath him. He thought that the whale was going to kill him. But instead, the whale came up right in front of the diver near the surface and nudged the diver in the chest and pushed him back; she did this again and again. The whale then rose up a bit more to the surface and looked into the face of the diver and just stared at him for a while. She then left him and went to one of the other divers and did the exact same thing. Then she went to a third diver and did the same thing. She did it with all the divers. She then went to the boat and did the same thing.

In fact, the divers and the boat had to leave because she wasn't willing to leave them.[35] Those divers risked their own well-being for the whale, and it made a difference to both the whale, to the divers, and maybe even to those who have heard or read about it.

A connection between the divers and the whale was forged that day. The divers said they never forgot about this experience. In fact, they reported that it changed their lives. These divers may not be considered bodhisattvas under its traditional definition. Who can really say what was in their hearts and minds? However, they were willing to go beyond self-centeredness and open their hearts to the suffering of another being.

The way to connect with others is by putting ourselves at risk, not physically, but by opening our hearts, which may seem as risky as cutting ropes from a giant whale. Indeed, it may take a great amount of courage to open our hearts to everyone. Like the whale, we are bound by the ropes of habit and fear. Many people are barely holding on, barely able to breathe, and are constantly being pulled down by the weight of fear. As a response, they inadvertently close themselves off in hopes of protecting themselves. To free ourselves from these ropes, we can open our hearts. They may only loosen a little in the beginning, but over time, they might just break open completely, and we may find we have fallen in love with all beings.

Openhearted acts are not just for heroes who put their lives at risk to save another. Another kind of hero is someone who can witness the suffering of the world and be open to seeing; someone who can listen with an open heart, offer a hand, share the bounty of their efforts, be present, show genuine concern—someone to send loving thoughts towards those who are suffering. These acts, albeit less dramatic than saving a whale, have meaning for the recipients. They also have a profound impact on those willing to open up. By opening our hearts, we are transforming our relationship to the world. Indeed, the greatest impact may be on ourselves.

As we look around with the eyes of a bodhisattva, we see the need for love and compassion: a man sleeping on a picnic bench, a mother yelling at her child in the store, an old lady struggling to get out of her car, a driver honking and cursing, people who are hungry, enslaved, mistreated, and those who have everything yet are still suffering. With openheartedness and courage, we become a witness to the human condition. To witness means to not be overcome by what we see but to be willing to look, to not turn away, and be present for all the manifestations of life. This includes being a witness to our own confusion, sadness, fear, and anger.

One day while dropping my husband off at the airport, I observed the occupants of a car that had pulled in behind me at the curb. The car caught and held my attention because there was a woman driving and a man sitting in the back seat. No one else was in the car. The woman had a very unhappy look on her face. The man got out of the car and scrambled to get all of his stuff out of the backseat and onto the curb which took him a little while. He seemed to be a bit harried, so the task didn't appear to be easy for him. During this time the woman never looked back at the man. Finally, he closed the back door of the car but before he could move, the woman pulled away from the curb, never looking back or saying a word. The man squatted down on the sidewalk as he watched her drive away with a look of complete and utter devastation.

I don't know if they were romantically involved, brother and sister, or if he was a hitchhiker. He continued to squat there on the sidewalk with a heartbreaking look. As I watched her pull away, she had an equally heartbreaking look on her face. It was like a tragic scene out of a romantic movie. It looked so very painful, and there was nothing I could do to fix the situation, but I could witness it and even send wishes for peace and joy to return to the couple.

Bodhisattvas work towards awakening and benefiting beings. To live with an awakened heart, we face suffering, both our own and that of others, rather than closing ourselves off to it. Experiencing our own suffering helps us to bring about a wish to relieve the suffering of others. When we have insight into the nature of our own suffering, we become motivated to not only free ourselves but to go beyond limited views and include all beings. "Our longing to be free from suffering is simply the longing of all that lives to be free from suffering." This is transcendent wisdom as expressed in the *Transcendent Wisdom Sutra*.[36] Instead of limiting our love and compassion only to those close to us, we can begin by developing universal love and compassion that won't discriminate between those we are close to and those we consider strangers.

A rather famous figure in Buddhism, Shantideva, an Indian master, is considered to have been a bodhisattva. He encouraged us to include everyone in our hearts and care for them as we would care for ourselves. He said that all beings can be seen as extensions of ourselves. Just as we reach out to soothe a part of us when we hurt, we can reach out to care for others.[37]

Love and compassion are needed now more than ever because there is so much suffering in the world. We are all interconnected, no longer isolated from one another in our own small communities. Many of us have become accustomed to limiting our love and compassion only to those we are close to, like our families and friends. We consider ourselves strangers to one another because we don't think we know anything about one another. We don't know the names of each other's children or share joys and sorrows together. However, we all share commonalities, the foremost of which is that we are sentient beings, and as such we share the desire to avoid suffering. We all want love and happiness. Our neighbors, those on the other side of town or the other side of the world, all want to live happy lives. The rice farmer in Indonesia, the bureaucrat in Washington, and the warrior in the Sudan, all want the same thing you and I want. We may seem to be light years apart, but when we look beyond these conceptual limits, we can find our common humanity. We can see ourselves as a part of the family of sentient beings.

It may not even occur to us to have compassion towards others until there is a tragedy. If we witness an accident or a natural disaster, we often feel strong feelings of empathy and compassion for those who are suffering. In the past, we have seen a great outpouring of generosity when tragedies like 9/11, a mass shooting, a tsunami, or an earthquake kills many people. At these times, our hearts open and we experience a strong connection to those who suffer and naturally want to relieve their suffering. Sometimes people will jump into their car or board an airplane to do what they can to alleviate the suffering they have witnessed from afar. We give our money, time, prayers, and resources. An overwhelming desire arises to help in some way; we simply can't stand by without doing something. Tragedy often results in an outpouring of goodwill and generosity. At these times, we not only see our interconnection, but also gain insight into the nature of suffering. Our priorities may even realign as we examine our own lives and the thin thread that connects us to them and to those we love.

Yet for many, after time passes, the realization of our interconnectedness fades into the background, and we fall back into our habits of separation, self-grasping, and again limit our concern for only those closest to us. However, if we make living with an awakened heart our life's activity, we will not forget to care for all beings.

Maybe we can't save the world, but what we do for even one being can make a big difference. Families of Jews hiding in sewers in Poland, during World War II, were helped by an ordinary man who brought them food and medicine at great risk to himself.[38] A man in a New York City subway station who witnessed a stranger fall onto the tracks with a train bearing down on him jumped on top of him to save him with only a half an inch to spare between them and the train that passed over them.[39] In Utah, several people jumped in to lift a burning car in order to save a trapped motorcyclist.[40] Because of what these people did in a spontaneous act of love and compassion, family members of the victims were able to enjoy their loved ones a little longer, and the victims themselves were able to live longer lives. Who knows the impact of saving one person's life? Of course, we all won't be put into the position to literally save a person's life as those I just described. But, all of us can open our hearts to the suffering of others.

When I was a child, I remember driving on the freeway heading back to Los Angeles from San Diego, and as was often the case, we were stuck in traffic. After some time passed and we inched forward, we came upon the cause of the traffic, a horrible accident which included several people thrown out of a vehicle. I didn't actually see this accident and can only relate what I have heard because when we came upon this scene, my mother said, "Dana, close your eyes and don't open them until I tell you." My mother didn't want me to see what I probably would not have been able to process.

Unlike young children, we can train ourselves to be a witness to all of life and engage in actions that benefit beings as we mature in our meditation practice. We can learn to open our eyes, our hearts, and our minds and live with an awakened heart. Through bodhichitta, we can be touched by the fullness of life. We can open our hearts to the beauty of the world, to all beings, and to that from which we would normally turn away. In doing so, our practice becomes more informed by wisdom, and eventually, we see the emptiness of the self, others, and all experience.

12

The Extraordinary
in the Ordinary

Throughout our lives, we open many doors hoping that joy will be found just across the threshold. We may spend most of our lives working towards this goal. We may read self-help books trying to fix something wrong with us and strategize about how to overcome a sense of disconnection. Or, we may try to control the world around us in an attempt to align it with our ideas about how it should be. However, none of these strategies really work long term.

I've tried some of these strategies myself. When I buy one thing, I find I want two things; when I think I've found the one thing or person that will bring me lasting joy, I've found it is temporary. This pattern has been repeated time after time with the same result. Someone once told me that her life would be complete when she had a tennis bracelet and a Mercedes. Years ago, she ended up getting both of these things, but she no longer has either of them and has even purchased and sold four cars since that time. I guess she didn't find that completeness with a bracelet and a car. Isn't it funny how we continue to do the same thing again and again and are no closer to our goal? Even with these various approaches to finding joy, we continually miss the gateway to a joyous life.

Harry Potter who searched the train station looking for platform 9 3/4 to access the train to Hogwarts, missed seeing what was right in front of him. To everyone in the train station, except those who have been to Hogwarts before, there wasn't a platform 9 3/4. Where the entrance should have been was a brick wall. No one would even think to look for a doorway in a seemingly solid brick wall, but that is where platform 9 3/4 was, sitting in plain sight.[41] Like this, the door that leads beyond dissatisfaction is blocked from our view, yet is in plain sight. The entrance sometimes needs to be pointed out to us.

I had the chance to travel in England using the London Underground, more fondly known as the Tube, to travel throughout the city. Whenever the train door opened I'd hear, "Mind the gap." Yet, every time the door opened, there was only the smallest of gaps between the train and the platform. It made me wonder why the persistent announcement was necessary because the gap was so small. Near the end of the week as I traveled further into the city, the doors opened and the usual "Mind the gap" announcement ricocheted off the interior of the London Underground station. As I made my way towards the doors to exit the train, I noticed a big gap between the train and the platform. I didn't have to leap across it, but it was significant enough to require a warning, and the announcement finally became relevant. Thankfully, the gap was pointed out again and again,

Many Buddhist masters also point out a gap to their students; however, this gap is a bit more subtle, much more subtle than the small gap I initially noticed between the train and the platform. It is a gap between our thoughts. When looking at our minds, we may not notice there's a gap between each thought. It may take us a while to see it, but this gap is always there. As the persistent announcement on the train seemed irrelevant at first, this talk about a gap may not seem very relevant at first, but eventually we will see its importance. The reason this gap is important is because of its unconditioned nature. This gap is not a "thing"—it is naked awareness.

How is it naked? To start, we could say it's empty of problems, confusion, striving, sadness, desire, sorrow, grasping, and clinging. Indeed, it is also empty of all other concepts. It's pure suchness, which is indefinable, so to know it requires a direct experience of it. When residing in that space, there's a natural joy that arises. There's a natural gratefulness that arises. There's a natural love and compassion that arises. So, it's empty, but is also luminous and clear. When we let go of our conditioned minds, we can experience this for ourselves.

I used to commute to college through the Palouse, a vast farming area of rolling hills. Lush green and yellow fields of rapeseed were set alongside wispy stalks of wheat, bowing with the breeze, swaying back and forth, making the landscape appear like a moving ocean of vibrant color. In the fall, some of the fields are burned, which replaces nutrients in the soil. In early spring, the tractors turn up the rich, dark soil, clearing out weeds and preparing for seeds to be planted. Beginning in the early summer months, the fields are filled with wheat, grasses, and rapeseed. The vistas are so breathtakingly beautiful that drivers often feel a strong urge to pull over and sit with the beauty that extends as far as the eye can see. To me, it is a place so beautiful and vast that it stops the mind. When this happens, it is possible to experience simple, yet profound, awareness.

The Buddha talked about plowing the field of the mind. By tilling the soil of the mind, we clear out the weeds of concepts that encumber it and allow space for the seeds of wisdom to flourish. The field is plowed in order to make a place for wisdom to arise. When we have a lot of mental clutter, it is difficult for us to see our true nature. Resting in the natural state of the mind clears out the mental weeds of our concepts. Through simple awareness, the weeds of concepts are burned, and unencumbered awareness is left.

Because we don't recognize the freedom that is in the palm of our hands, often a teacher will point out the nature of the mind to a disciple. Patrul Rinpoche, a Tibetan Buddhist master, had a close disciple by the name of Nyoshul Lungtok. When they first met, Nyoshul Lungtok asked Patrul Rinpoche for instructions on the nature of the mind. With the wisdom of a great master, rather than giving him these instructions right away, Patrul Rinpoche told him to stay with him for a while. Nyoshul Lungtok ended up staying with Patrul Rinpoche for twenty-eight years. The story is told that one night Patrul Rinpoche lay on the ground and asked Nyoshul Lungtok to lie on the ground beside him. When he did, Patrul Rinpoche instructed him to look up at the night sky and then asked him a series of questions: Do you see the stars up in the sky? Do you hear dogs barking in the monastery? Do you hear my voice? Nyoshul Lungtok answered yes to all of Patrul Rinpoche's questions. He could see the stars in the sky, hear the dog barking, and hear Patrul Rinpoche's voice. Then Patrul

Rinpoche pointed out that what Nyoshul Lungtok was experiencing in that moment was the nature of mind itself.[42]

This was an ordinary night: stars were in the sky, a dog was barking in the distance, Patrul Rinpoche was speaking, yet what Nyoshul Lungtok experienced as Patrul Rinpoche pointed out the ordinary was a profound and lasting understanding of the nature of mind. Nyoshul Lungtok wasn't trying to do anything, yet he experienced unfabricated, pristine awareness while residing in the natural state of mind.

Because of our conditioned view of things, we might expect liberation to contain fireworks and the "Hallelujah Chorus." This is a misunderstanding. As with Nyoshul Lungtok, the experience is extraordinary yet ordinary. Mental fireworks and the "Hallelujah Chorus" are temporary experiences; they are not the truth itself.

To experience the truth for ourselves, we don't need the use of physical tools like telescopes, Hadron Colliders, mathematical formulas, or the manipulation of atoms. All we need for our investigation is the awareness we already possess. We can begin by minding the gap, recognizing the natural state of the mind, and over time we can hang out in the natural state of awareness.

When we meditate, we are not trying to make anything happen or fall into a special state. We are simply resting in the natural state of awareness. In some sense, it is an act of nondoing, nonmeditation. Awareness is always with us; in fact, it is us. Like the stars in the sky at noon that are obscured by the brilliance of the sun, but are always present, uncontrived awareness is always present, yet is hidden from view to the untrained mind. Through insight, we can experience the extraordinary display of suchness in any ordinary moment. The nature of the mind is intrinsically aware, and if we don't hold onto anything with our mind, we can experience this flow of awareness.

By resting in the natural state of awareness, we have the opportunity to see what is naturally present, to awaken from the conditioned into the unconditioned, from the confused mind into the enlightened mind, from the small to the big. It is to be fully enlivened, untied from our habits and conditioning. We can unchain ourselves from this very conditioned existence. Awareness is not based on causes and conditions—it is inherently present. In other words, we don't need to *do* anything; indeed, doing gets in the way. This is why the great masters have instructed us to simply rest. They observed that if we leave the mind in its naturally clear state without accepting or rejecting what appears, the mind is liberated. Padmasambhava, who is credited with the dispersion of Buddhism in Tibet, indicated, "When intrinsic awareness remains in its own space, it is quite ordinary and in no way exceptional. This awareness that is present and lucidly clear is called by the name of ordinary awareness."[43]

We don't need to *make* our moments extraordinary or special, nor do we need to search out entertainment, altered states of mind, vacations, and the like. Of course, it is fine to do these things, we just need to know their temporary nature. We can experience naked awareness at our kitchen table or at the dump, because outer conditions don't have anything to do with the experience of awareness itself. It is always accessible because it is present in every moment. If we stop and look inward, we may be able to experience this for ourselves.

We will need consistent repetition to stay with awareness. At first, our minds are wild like a raging river, but through training they eventually become wide open. In the beginning, the problem is we believe in our thoughts. Later, we try to use other thoughts to free ourselves from thoughts. Eventually, we may see that the nature of the mind is like space and thoughts are appearances like rainbows. They appear based on causes and conditions and disappear when those causes and conditions aren't present. Thoughts have no inherent existence. They appear in the sky of the mind, and when left alone, they dissolve.

By resting in naked awareness, the knot of conceptual mind undoes itself. We are able to rest in the midst of both the silence and the storms of our minds. Within this awareness, the essence of samsara (the cycle of suffering) and nirvana (the extinguishment of suffering) are not separate. The idea of a separation only arises within a confused dualistic mind. In fact, there isn't a me being aware; there is only awareness. When the pristine sky of the mind appears, we experience the nature of reality. From the perspective of the absolute there isn't even a hair's breadth of separation between the ordinary and the extraordinary. Finally, everything is seen for what it is, already naturally and extraordinarily free.

Notes

Introduction

1. Sharon Salzberg, "Reclaiming Our Power," in *A Heart as Wide as the World: Stories on the Path of Lovingkindness* (Boston: Shambhala Publications, 1999), 20.

Chapter One

2. Doreen A. Diego, "Depression: The Parable of the Boiling Frog," *American Bar Association Newsletter*, January 1, 2008, http://www.americanbar.org/newsletter/publications /gp_solo_magazine_home/ gp_solo_magazine_index/2008_jan_feb_inthesolution.html.

3. "C. G. Jung, Quotes," Goodreads, accessed September 12, 2014, https://www.goodreads .com/author/quotes/38285.C_G_Jung.

4. James Garbarino, "An American Story," in *The Future, As If It Really Mattered* (Longmont, CO: Bookmakers Guild, 1988).

Chapter Two

5. Liz Osborn, "Number of Species Identified on Earth," *Current Results: Research News and Science Facts*, 2014, http://www. currentresults.com/Environment-Facts/Plants-Animals /number-species.php.

6. Rachael Nuwer, "How Many Species of Cockroaches Plague Humanity?" *Smithsonian.com*, December 11, 2013, http:// www.smithsonianmag.com/smart-news/how-many-species-of -cockroaches-plague-humanity 180948133/?no-ist.

7. "Heraclitus," BrainyQuote.com, accessed September 11, 2014, http://www.brainyquote.com /quotes/quotes/h/heraclitus107157. html.

Chapter Three

8. "Ludwig Wittgenstein," BrainyQuote.com, accessed September 18, 2014, http://www. brainyquote.com/quotes/quotes/l/ ludwigwitt134835.html.

9. Lex Hixon, *Mother of the Buddhas: Meditation on the Prajnaparamita Sutra* (Wheaton, Illinois:Quest, 1993), 121–122.

Chapter Four

10. Hixon, *Mother of the Buddhas*, 39.

Chapter Five

11. Melissa Ller and Reinhard Piechocki, *A Garden of Eden in Hell: The Life of Alice Herz-Sommer* (London: Macmillan, 2007).

12. "Theodore Isaac Rubin," BrainyQuote.com, accessed September 2014, http://www. brainyquote.com/quotes/quotes/t/ theodoreis380693.html.

13. Shantideva, "Patience," in *The Way of the Bodhisattva: A Translation of the Bodhicharyāvatāra* (Boston: Shambhala Publications, 1997), 79.

14. Susan Martinez-Conde and Stephen L. Macknik, "The Neuroscience of Illusion: How Tricking the Eye Reveals the Inner Workings of the Brain," *Scientific American Special Edition*, 22, no. 3 (New York: Scientific American, 2013):6.

15. Stephen Macknik and S. Conde, *Sleights of Mind: What the Neuroscience of Magic Reveals about Our Brains* (London: Profile, 2011), 84-85.

16. Daisetz Teitaro Suzuki, *The Lankavatara Sutra: A Mahayana Text, Verse 160*, trans. Daisetz Teitaro Suzuki (London: Routledge and K. Paul, 1966), 84.

17. Chogyam Trungpa, "Transformation of Bad Circumstances into the Path of Enlightenment," in *Training the Mind and Cultivating Loving-kindness*, ed. Judith L. Lief (Boston: Shambhala Publications, 1993), 49.

18. "Two Questions, Part II, Having to Do with Dandelions," The Outrageous Wisdom of Nasruddin, accessed February 3, 2013, http://www.nasruddin.org/pages/stories /twoquestions2.html.

19. Christina Lundberg, "For the Benefit of Beings: The Extraordinary Life of His Eminence Garchen Triptrul Rinpoche,"

directed by Christina Lundberg (Garuda Sky Publications, 2013). DVD.

20. Gochen Tulku Rinpoche (Sang-Ngag Tenzin), "A Brief Autobiographical Account from the Words of Gochen Tulku Rinpoche, Sang-Ngag Tenzin," June 8, 2000. 3-4, http://www. ewam.org/wp-content/uploads/2012/04/Rinpoche-Autobiography. pdf.

Chapter Six

21. Dilgo Khyentse, "The Commentary," in *The Heart of Compassion: The Thirty-Seven Verses on the Practice of a Bodhisattva: A Commentary* (Boston: Shambhala Publications, 2007), 129.

22. Mark D. Seery, E. Alison Holman, and Roxane Cohen Silver, "Whatever Does Not Kill Us: Cumulative Lifetime Adversity, Vulnerability, and Resilience," *Journal of Personality and Social Psychology*, 99, no. 6, (December 2010): 1025–104114.

23. Kyle, "A Few Buddhist Parables," *Progressive Buddhism* (blog), April 7, 2009, http://progressivebuddhism.blogspot.com/2009/04/few-buddhist-parables.html.

24. Daniel Ladinsky, "Rabia," in *Love Poems from God: Twelve Sacred Voices from the East and West* (New York: Penguin Compass, 2002), 1–2.

25. Don Kaplan, "NBC's 'Dateline' Focuses on Young Oregon Family Whose Five Children Have Deadly Heart Disease," *NY Daily News,* June 4, 2013, http://www.nydailynews.com /entertainment/ tv-movies/nbc-dateline-focuses-family-children-deadly-heart-disease-article -1.1362090.

26. Sonam Rinchen Geshe and Ruth Sonam, "Dreams and Rainbows," in *The Thirty-Seven Practices of Bodhisattvas: An Oral Teaching*, 1st ed. (Ithica: Snow Lion Publications, 1997), 24.

Chapter Eight

27. Sandra Blakeslee and Matthew Blakeslee, "The Embodied Brain," in *The Body Has a Mind of Its Own: New Discoveries about How the Mind-Body Connection Helps Us Master the World* (New York: Random House, 2008), 4.

28. Ellen Horne Producer Series, hosted by Robert Krulwichis and Jad Abumrad, "Where Is the Part That Is Me?," *Who Am I?*, Radiolab, NPR, WNYC, February 4, 2005, radio broadcast, http://www.radiolab.org/story/91496-who-am-i/.

29. Dalai Lama, "The Nature and Existence of Self," in *Practicing Wisdom: The Perfection of Shantideva's Bodhisattva Way, Verse 74* (Boston: Wisdom Publications, 2004), 105.

Chapter Nine

30. Ladinsky, "Rumi," 69.

Chapter Ten

31. Kyle, "The Search for Enlightenment,"

32. Hixon, *Mother of the Buddhas*, 34.

33. Machik Labdön, *Machik's Complete Explanation: Clarifying the Meaning of Chod*, trans. and ed. Sarah Harding, Expanded Edition (Ithica, NY: Snow Lion Publications, 2003), 229–230.

34. Dakpo Tashi Namgyal, "The Relevant Meditation on Insight," in *Mahāmudrā the Moonlight Quintessence of Mind and Meditation*, trans. by Lobsang Phuntshok Lhalungpa, 2nd ed. (Somerville: Wisdom Publications, 2006), 199.

Chapter Eleven

35. Ellen Horne Producer Series, hosted by Robert Krulwichis and Jad Abumrad, "Animal Minds," *Animal Blessings*, Radiolab, NPR, WNYC, April 11, 2010, radio broadcast, http://www.radiolab.org/story/91701-animal-minds/.

36. Hixon, *Mother of the Buddhas*, 47.

37. Shantideva, *The Way of the Bodhisattva: A Translation of the Bodhicharyā vatā ra*, *Verse 91,* trans. Padmakara Translation Group (Boston: Shambhala Publications, 1997), 123.

38. Marshall, Robert. *In the Sewers of Lvov: The Last Sanctuary from the Holocaust*. 2nd ed. (London: Bloomsbury Reader, 2013).

39. Cara Buckley, "A Man Down, a Train Arriving, and a Stranger Makes a Choice," *The New York Times*, January 2, 2007, http://www.nytimes.com/2007/01/03/nyregion /03life.html?_r=0.

40. "Motorcyclist's Uncle Tells Nephew's Rescuers, 'You Are Heroes,'" CNN Justice, accessed September 13, 2011, http://www.cnn.com/2011/CRIME/09/13/utah.motorcycle.crash/

Chapter Twelve

41. Rowling, J. K. "The Journey from Platform Nine and Three-quarters." In Harry Potter and the Sorcerer's Stone. 1st ed. New York: Scholastic, 1998.

42. Sogyal Rinpoche, *The Tibetan Book of Living and* Dying, ed. Patrick Gaffney and Andrew Harvey (San Francisco: HarperCollins Publishers, 2002), 160.

43. John Myrdhin Reynolds, "Translation of the Text," in *Self-Liberation through Seeing with Naked Awareness* (Ithaca: Snow Lion Publications, 2010), 22.

About the Author

Dana Marsh, M.A. is an American Buddhist Dharma teacher who was ordained in the Nyingma lineage by Tibetan Lama Anam Thubten Rinpoche, after many years of meditation practice and study under his guidance. She encourages and guides others with love, humor, and devotion to the truth, to experience nonconceptual transcendent wisdom. She is the resident teacher of Heart of the Dharma Sangha in Boise, Idaho, providing an avenue for spiritual seekers to meet with the liberating wisdom teachings from the Buddhist tradition. Her teaching style is easy to relate to and contemporary, she invites everyone to see their own beautiful nature.

You can learn more about Dana's activities by joining her mailing list, visiting her website, or sending inquiries directed to:

Heart of the Dharma
P. O. Box 7035
Boise, ID 83707

www.heartofdharma.org
www.compassioninsight.org

CPSIA information can be obtained at www.ICGtesting.com
Printed in the USA
BVOW07s1714161114

375202BV00001B/2/P